BEST SHORT HIKES™ in

Washington's
NORTH CASCADES
& SAN JUAN ISLANDS

E. M. STERLING
PHOTOS BY BOB & IRA SPRING

THE MOUNTAINEERS BOOKS

Marmot

All of the camps include parking and tent areas, picnic tables, and fire pits. All have at least pit toilets. Water is available if indicated.

Space in the campgrounds, however, is not assured. Single and group campsites can be reserved in advance by telephone in some Washington State Parks and in some National Forest Service campgrounds. Group sites can also be reserved by phone in some National Forest campgrounds (see Appendix 2, Information Sources).

Most of the unreserved campsites are likely to be filled on weekends and holidays. Best opportunities occur midweek before or after school vacation periods.

Many non-fee camps do not provide garbage services. In such camps take your garbage home. Please, take your garbage home.

And lest we forget: Remember how far sound carries in the woods. Keep your radio turned down, and remember that 10 p.m. is bedtime in every camp.

BACKPACKING

Many of the hikes here offer opportunities for short overnight backpack trips. Few, however, lead to spots that suggest prolonged vacations.

Backpack books (see Appendix 3, Reading Suggestions) provide details on packs, cooking gear, sleeping bags, tents, and the like. Suffice it to say here that a short hike provides an opportunity to test your equipment, particularly if you have children along. For failure and even catastrophe will leave you only 2 miles or less from your car.

Overnight camping permits are required in most backcountry areas.

ENJOY (AND LEARN)

Enjoy, most certainly. But, more importantly, beyond pleasure, look around as you drive to or walk through the places listed here. See and try to understand.

First, in the lower valleys logged long ago, note how much of the summer green is brush and alders and how little of it is actually regrowing conifers, of the kind that once grew there.

Later, as your road climbs higher, pay attention to the clear-cuts, new and old, and wonder at what you see. When you pass a sign that says "replanted" this year or that, or even if the clear-cut is not signed, look closely at what commercial foresters call "reforestation."

Fix the picture in your mind, and when you finally get to some small, ancient, unlogged forest compare and wonder. Will those replanted forests stocked as advertised with two seedlings for every old

Tiger lily on the Sauk Mountain trail

tree logged ever—ever—equal the uncut old forests you now enjoy? And next, would the forest you see recover more certainly, and more grandly, if other methods—"practices" of logging, as they say—had been carried out?

And note, too, when you reach your trailhead how closely logging borders sometimes intrude on many of the sanctuaries here. Note how often you can see clear-cuts through the trees and, in noting, wonder what impact those cleared areas will have, or are having, on the "preserved" forest in which you walk. From wind damage along the now-unprotected forest borders over time? From changes in wildlife patterns caused by the nearby removal of all the trees? On once-resident birds, rodents, deer, or bear? On snowfall runoff in the spring? On the retention of rainfall in the summer? On the mix of plants over time? Rest assured as you make your guess that nobody else knows the answers either.

And note often how suddenly everything changes around you as you step beyond the signs that say "wilderness" or "park." Sometimes like night to day. You could almost ask: Who needs the sign?

More importantly, as you wander past or through the forests here, whether on state, federal, or private lands, remember: You are the keeper of all these forests. What happens to all of them depends on you.

You have a personal interest, and a right to have an interest, in every clear-cut, road, unlogged area, replanted site, wilderness, lake, waterfall, and river that you see. These forests are yours to manage. Every one of them.

Your role in what you see in public forests—state or federal—is clear. You own them. It's your money being spent. Your policies being carried out. You—yes, you—deserve the credit for what is good, and you also deserve the blame for what is bad. For you have received exactly what you asked for. And if you didn't ask? Who else is there to blame?

And on private forests? On those huge, ugly, logged-off blocks of railroad land. Trees—most of them—cut and shipped to Asia. You're responsible for those forests, too.

Private forests, throughout all of the nations of the Western world, including those in Washington, are forests awarded to private owners to be held and used in trust for you. The public here (in Europe, it was once the sovereign king) has, and always has had, the right, the power, the obligation to demand that forests—all forests—be managed in the public (in your, the sovereign's) interest all the time.

And for all sorts of ancient and modern reasons. And all of them so basic they are sometimes overlooked. Forests are necessary for all people—in the nation, in the world—for housing, recreation, stability of the soil, avalanche control, water retention, weather, even air quality, along with the survival of birds, plants, and animals—just to begin a list.

Therefore, it's in your individual undisputed public interest—as the guardian of all forests in a democracy—to impose and enforce all necessary logging practices, controls, and restraints. And to impose them as you, the sovereign dispenser of all forest rights, think they should be in your (the public's) greatest interest.

Yes, enjoy what you find here. But, please, accept responsibility for protecting all the beauty that you see.

AND FINALLY: BE WARNED

Don't take any of the 105 trails listed here for granted. Enjoy all of them but remember any and all of them can be taken away.

Most of the trails covered here have some level of government protection. Many of them cross or end in legally designated national and state parks, national wilderness areas, or national recreation areas. Some in National Forests have been set aside as "nature trails." All seemingly dedicated to recreation use.

But the governments or government agencies that give protection can also take it away. And the pressure on them to so does not cease. The land crossed by trails here contain valuable timber, gold, other minerals, and thousands of acres of recreation real estate, all with a need for logging roads, mining roads, highways, oil wells, and all the other "benefits and necessities of development" in all its forms.

So, when you hike any of the trails here, enjoy the flowers, the great trees, the grand vistas, the brisk air, the cold water, the beaver's house, the bear's tracks, the birds' songs. Take pictures of everything you see. And if you hear that the government or some agency plans to destroy what you've seen: Raise hell! Complain to every government official that you know of. In the strongest, most detailed language you can muster. And join with any organization that's willing to state your case. Remain silent and you will have given away all the wonders your grandchildren also might enjoy. The power is yours. But you must use it.

—*E. M. Sterling*

Grouse in Heather Meadows

A NOTE ABOUT SAFETY

Safety is an important concern in all outdoor activities. No guidebook can alert you to every hazard or anticipate the limitations of every reader. Therefore, the descriptions of roads, trails, routes, and natural features in this book are not representations that a particular place or excursion will be safe for your party. When you follow any of the routes described in this book, you assume responsibility for your own safety. Under normal conditions, such excursions require the usual attention to traffic, road and trail conditions, weather, terrain, the capabilities of your party, and other factors. Additionally, some of the lands in this book may experience development and/or change of ownership. Conditions may change, making use of some of these routes unwise. Always check for current conditions, respect posted private property signs, and avoid confrontations with property owners or managers. Keeping informed on current conditions and exercising common sense are the keys to a safe, enjoyable outing.

—*The Mountaineers Books*

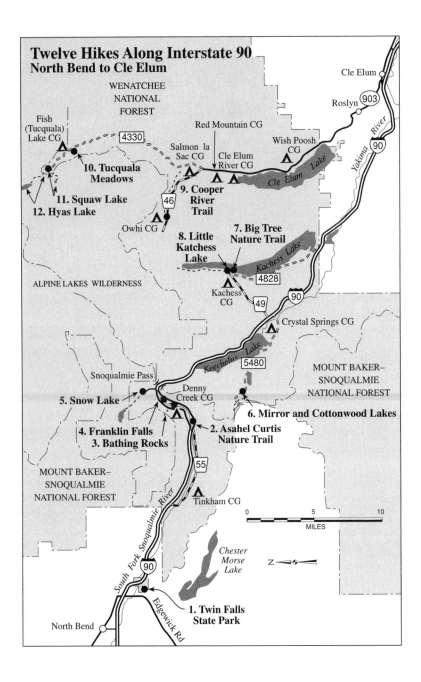

Twelve Hikes Along Interstate 90
North Bend to Cle Elum

Cle Elum

Roslyn 903

WENATCHEE
NATIONAL
FOREST

Fish
(Tucquala)
Lake CG

4330

Red Mountain CG

Salmon la
Sac CG

Cle Elum
River CG

Wish Poosh
CG

Cle Elum Lake

Yakima River

90

**10. Tucquala
Meadows**

11. Squaw Lake
12. Hyas Lake

46

**9. Cooper
River
Trail**

Owhi CG

**8. Little
Katchess
Lake**

**7. Big Tree
Nature Trail**

Kachess Lake

4828

ALPINE LAKES WILDERNESS

Kachess
CG

49

90

Crystal Springs CG

Keechelus Lake

5480

MOUNT BAKER–
SNOQUALMIE
NATIONAL FOREST

Snoqualmie Pass

5. Snow Lake

Denny
Creek CG

6. Mirror and Cottonwood Lakes

4. Franklin Falls
3. Bathing Rocks

**2. Asahel Curtis
Nature Trail**

55

MOUNT BAKER–
SNOQUALMIE
NATIONAL FOREST

South Fork Snoqualmie River

Tinkham CG

0   5   10
MILES

N

Chester
Morse
Lake

90

**1. Twin Falls
State Park**

Edgewick Rd

North Bend

Tucquala Lake in the upper Salmon la Sac Valley

TWELVE HIKES ALONG INTERSTATE 90

NORTH BEND TO CLE ELUM

Any of the hikes in this section offers an easy one-day sample of what hikers can find from spring through fall.

Don't miss the waterfalls at **Twin Falls State Park** (Hike 1) or the grand old-growth forest along the **Asahel Curtis Nature Trail** (Hike 2). With children, enjoy the natural water slide at **Bathing Rocks** (Hike 3). Join lots of hikers on the trail to **Snow Lake** (Hike 5). Meander through the summer-long rich display of wild flowers on **Tucquala Meadows** (Hike 10), or savor the grand scenery on the way to **Squaw Lake** (Hike 11).

For information on campgrounds nearby, see Appendix 1, Campgrounds. To obtain updated reports on trail and road conditions, contact the Washington State Parks Information Center, the North Bend and Cle Elum Rangers Stations, and see the Mount Baker–Snoqualmie National Forest website listed in Appendix 2.

1. TWIN FALLS STATE PARK

Features	▪	fine forest and two waterfalls
One way	▪	about 1 mile
Elevation gain	▪	200 feet
Difficulty	▪	moderate
Open	▪	all year
Map	▪	Green Trails 206

As you walk this lovely trail, take note: it almost didn't turn out that way.

At one point a private electric power company proposed to build an ugly powerhouse in the middle of the park where great ancient trees still stand. Conservationists objected to the plan. As a result of the protest the company imaginatively changed its plan and instead of building a powerhouse put all of its generating machinery in a tunnel out of sight or sound beneath the park.

So before you leave the waterfalls, remember it was activists like you who wrote letters and showed up at the hearings that led the company to develop the underground solution that so perfectly solved the problem.

Drive east on I-90 past North Bend, turn right at Edgewick Exit 34 and right again on Edgewick Road, and drive south to SE 159th Street. Turn left and drive to the end of the street in 1 mile.

The trail leaves the upriver end of the parking lot and wanders through rich forest for 0.5 mile or more before turning uphill to a viewpoint and then beyond to spur trails leading to viewing platforms of the lower falls.

At the end of a mile, the path drops through boulders in a rainforest-like setting, kept moist by spray from the falls, to a bridge across the river above the lower falls.

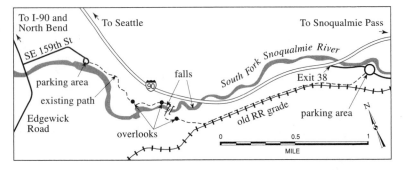

Views up and down the river here. Hike on another 25 yards or so, up two short spurts of trail and a burst of steps, to the base of a great old Douglas fir for a head-on view of the upper falls.

The path continues up through more forest, along the edge of a clear-cut, and down a powerline road to another parking area uphill to the right off I-90 Exit 38. A modest above-the-ground powerhouse across from the parking lot on the river here dominates a small waterfall that is hardly worth the visit.

Twin Falls

2. ASAHEL CURTIS NATURE TRAIL

Features ■	lush old-growth forest
One way ■	a short 1-mile loop
Elevation gain ■	slight
Difficulty ■	easy
Open ■	spring through fall
Map ■	Green Trails 207

The entrance sign says this grove of ancient trees contains about 140,000 board feet of lumber per acre. But ask yourself as you walk this trail: Does that total truly reflect the values here?

Drive east on I-90 and take Exit 47, turning right on Tinkham Road 55 at the end of the exit road. At a T intersection beyond the bridge over the Snoqualmie River, turn left on Forest Road 5590 to a large parking area at the end of the road. Find the nature trail to the left of the trail to Annette Lake.

(You can also reach this trail from the Asahel Curtis Picnic Area across the two-lane freeway. Trails near the river there lead through more rich forest, crossing beneath the freeway before climbing up to the parking area [above] and nature loop.)

The path immediately enters a lush forest of old Douglas fir marred only by the constant howl of trucks and cars rushing up the nearby highway.

Discounting the noise, you can see the grandeur the photographer Asahel Curtis saw here. Notice how this beleaguered patch of trees,

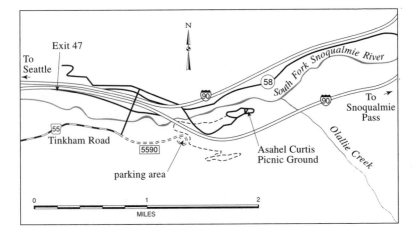

Humpback Creek, Asahel Curtis Nature Trail

unassisted, has sustained its growth for centuries and survives still, despite the assaults of speeding humans.

Note how old tumbled giants are survived by towering giants, themselves awaiting their time to fall, all surrounded by other trees of every size and shape and age waiting for their future moment in the sun. An evolving forest here for sure, one that, if left alone, will always display the grandeur of ancient trees.

But wonder which in the end will win. The highway? Or Nature's trees? Also wonder: If traffic needs increase, will these trees fall, too? Will the lumber extracted replace the value of what you see here now?

3. BATHING ROCKS

Features	▪	natural water slides
One way	▪	a long mile
Elevation gain	▪	500 feet
Difficulty	▪	moderate
Open	▪	summer
Map	▪	Green Trails 207

Walk through old forest along a pretty creek to a basking place with eroded chutes in polished rock where children and adults often shout and play.

Drive east on I-90, turn off at Exit 47, and cross left over the freeway and then right beyond the westbound entrance on Denny Creek Road 58. In about 2.5 miles pass Denny Creek Campground, turning left onto a road that crosses the river, passes some private homes, and ends at a large parking lot.

Take the Melakwa Lake Trail off the upper end of the parking loop.

The path starts above Denny Creek and then drops across a bridge before climbing beneath the freeway perched on stilts far above the trail, a European fashion that does little damage to the forest. In fact, except for the pops of vehicles crossing highway expansion joints, you may not hear the traffic here at all. An example, certainly, of what engineers can do when they want to avoid destruction of a mountainside in the construction of a freeway.

The trail levels off slightly as it continues to the Alpine Lakes Wilderness through more rich forest filled with ferns, berries, and flowers in their season.

Bathing rocks

Way paths lead to views down on some rock ledges before the trail crosses a log bridge over the creek to the popular rock water slides. The path straight ahead also leads to the water's edge but, when the stream is high, not to the other side.

The creek here, warmed by the sun and rocks, permits sliding in the tumbling water chutes all summer long, with a lot of places to picnic and watch from shoreside slabs.

And plan on a lot of activity on warm weekends. You won't believe the cross-section of young and old, fat and thin, you'll find hiking here to join children playing in the slippery chutes.

Hike upward beyond the crossing for another 0.5 mile to views of Keekwulee Falls and up another bunch of switchbacks to Snowshoe Falls.

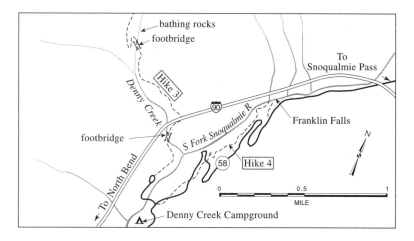

4. FRANKLIN FALLS

Features	▪	waterfall
One way	▪	0.25 mile or longer
Elevation gain	▪	slight
Difficulty	▪	moderate
Open	▪	whenever the road is free of snow
Map	▪	Green Trails 207

Take a short walk to what may be one of the most popular and accessible public waterfalls in Mount Baker–Snoqualmie National Forest. And then cheer that the water plunging over it was not diverted to a private power plant.

Franklin Falls

Drive east on I-90, turn off at Exit 47 and cross left over the freeway, and then turn right beyond the westbound entrance to Denny Creek Road 58. (See map on page 29.) For the shortest walk, drive a mile beyond Denny Creek Campground to a small parking area at the end of the third sharp switchback in the road. Find the trail off the road to the left.

Longer trails start at the bridge over Denny Creek off the access road to the Melakwa Lake Trail (see Hike 3, Bathing Rocks, for directions), or up the road to the second sharp switchback to a section of the Wagon Road Trail.

The shortest path drops sharply to the base of the falls, which plunges 70 feet over a cliff. In summer, rest awhile on a gravel bar at the base of the falls along with (on weekends) hordes of others.

Note while you are there how the freeway high above you impinges on the scene, destroying any sense of "forest" now. And then wonder what further impact a diversion of much of the river's water around the falls to a power plant would have had.

A private developer proposed to dam the river above the falls and divert water through pipes to a powerhouse on public land downstream. The Forest Service had decided that diversion of the river and construction of the powerhouse was not precluded by any of its regulations. The developer, however, withdrew from the project. No public hearings were held on the proposal.

5. SNOW LAKE

Features ■	high mountain lake
One way ■	3.5 miles
Elevation gain ■	1,700 feet
Difficulty ■	moderate to steep
Open ■	midsummer
Map ■	Green Trails 207

You can meet twenty to sixty people walking this trail with you on a weekday, even more on weekends. Yet the lake, at 4,016 feet, still remains one of the most beautiful places you can hike to so close to Seattle.

Drive east on I-90 to Snoqualmie Pass, turning off at Exit 52 and then left at the end of the exit road onto Alpental Road. Drive underneath the freeway and follow Alpental Road to its end in 1.5 miles in a parking area near a ski resort.

The trail starts up sharply off the upper right corner of the lot. It quickly enters a forest of handsome ancient mountain hemlocks, crosses an avalanche area strewn with huge trees mowed down by plunging snow, passes a small waterfall, and crosses still more rockfalls and avalanche chutes.

Snow Lake

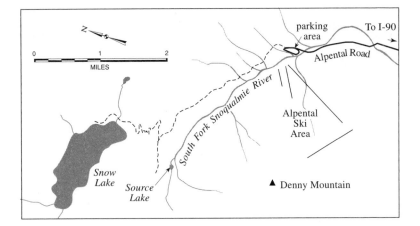

At 1.5 miles the trail, strewn each fall with fir cone cores stripped clean by chipmunks and Douglas squirrels, reaches a junction (a 0.5-mile trail left leads to a view down on Source Lake) and then starts switchbacking up a ridge. Higher and higher views back over the valley and Alpine Village as you climb. (Take care not to kick rocks downhill as you hike here: Others may be just below you.)

After some nine switchbacks the path enters the Alpine Lakes Wilderness and makes one last long traverse to the top of a ridge at 4,800 feet before starting down to the lake you see below.

The well-worn path, in heather meadows now, drops down four switchbacks across roots and rocks to spur paths leading to the cabin site you saw from the top of the ridge. No campfires permitted here.

Find your own viewing spot amid the meadows, creeks, and tarns, avoiding the areas marked with signs or blocked off by colored tapes put up to protect "restoration" areas from further overuse.

Some years more than 20,000 people in 200 cars make their way here between July and October. The yearly hordes so far have not destroyed the snow-laden peaks across the lake, but they have most certainly worn the groundcover bare in all of the most popular viewing spots, although—to give the warning signs their due—not as extensively as the damage might have been, as new growing trees around the cabin now attest.

The main path continues past a junction with a trail that goes over a ridge to the middle fork of the Snoqualmie and then 2 miles to Gem Lake and another 2 miles to Lower Wildcat Lake.

6. MIRROR AND COTTONWOOD LAKES

Features	■	two lakes on one trail
One way	■	1.25 miles
Elevation gain	■	600 feet
Difficulty	■	moderate to steep
Open	■	summer
Map	■	Green Trails 207

Two mountain lakes in a little over a mile, both set in rich old forest yet each of them different—and worthy of a visit.

Drive east on I-90 and turn off at Exit 62, just beyond Lake Keechelus and about 10 miles east from the top of Snoqualmie Pass.

Turn right onto Forest Road 54, cross the Yakima River, and turn right again on Forest Road 5480 in about 0.5 mile. Follow the road past Lost Lake. Turn right at a fork beyond the lake. Pause at the next left at the base of a steep, sometimes rough uphill spur and judge whether you should drive on or park and walk the last 0.5 mile to the trailhead.

The path starts out in a brushy clear-cut but, in 100 yards or less,

Mirror Lake and Tinkham Peak

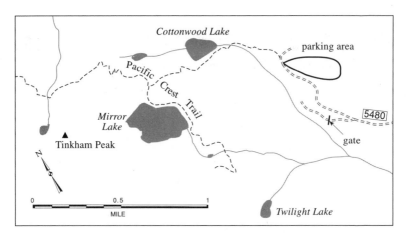

enters an old forest, following old blazes and crossing a creek before climbing sharply (but shortly) to Cottonwood Lake, the shallower of the two, at 3,900 feet. Stop here for sure before climbing higher (on switchbacks now) above Cottonwood Lake through a saddle to a heather meadow and a small tarn. Turn left on the Pacific Crest Trail to Mirror Lake, almost immediately to the right at 4,200 feet in its forest basin. The trail continues above the lake to the far end with a more open area in which to camp. Loiter here for sure.

7. BIG TREE NATURE TRAIL

Features	■	no more
One way	■	no more
Elevation gain	■	no more
Difficulty	■	no more
Open	■	not at all
Map	■	Green Trails 208

"No matter how long or far you've tramped in the Northwest mountains you'll not find a finer example of an old-growth forest at this elevation (2,500 feet) anywhere. Best early in the morning or on a summer evening . . . a cathedral built by Nature—just for you."
Best Short Hikes, *1994*

Sorry. The trail remains. The forest remains. Nature's cathedral is still there. But the hiking public is no longer invited to attend.

Big Tree Nature Trail

Identified as a public attraction in the 1960s, the trail was heavily used by the public and maintained by the Forest Service until 1998 when all of the trail and nature signs were quietly removed and the Cle Elum Ranger District, as a matter of policy, stopped talking about or maintaining the nature trail even though the public, if they knew about it, could still go there. Or so it was said. And so it still is.

If you would like to visit the trail, drive east on I-90 over Snoqualmie Pass, turning off at Exit 62 and turning left over the freeway to follow Forest Road 49 to the entrance of Kachess Campground in about 5 miles.

Since the district stopped talking about the trail, the grandeur of it remains but the opportunity to enjoy it has been totally destroyed. Plants have overgrown the paths and unstable windfalls lay where they landed, tottering over and across the trails and rolling anywhere and everywhere if disturbed. The number of the windfalls that fell across the loop trail is not known.

The windfalls, for the most part, have been sizable old trees weakened and then blown down after losing a natural battle with the much larger and stronger trees that still tower over the trail. As Ranger District authorities say, without maintenance the trail is unsafe and dangerous not only for hikers but for children from nearby campsites. Even though there are no warning signs anywhere around the former hiking loop.

Why the trail has not been maintained is not clearly explained. No pubic notice was given that the trail would be abandoned. The decision was made, the authorities say, based on a forest management plan that requires a "high degree of security, safety, and sanitary conditions" based on "established protocols for risk assessment." There is no evidence that the Ranger District prepared any estimates on the cost of stabilizing the area. Nor was any action taken to have the area considered as "a special area" provided for by Forest Service Regulations for small "areas that should be managed principally for recreation use substantially in their natural condition."

Yes, every wild forest presents a danger to every visitor. Mountain forests or mountain trails are not and never have been expected to be like city parks. The wildness of the Big Tree trail was the reason the trails and wildness were set aside.

But the windfall could be stabilized. The brush could be trimmed. The trails for the most part still exist. And the grandeur still remains.

If you now wonder as a reader why and what was done, contact the Cle Elm Ranger District (see Appendix 2) and ask. The public needs no permission to comment on the failures here. If you have a view, state it. It's your forest. Feel free to speak. And yes, write the Chief of the Forest Service, Dale Bosworth, P.O. Box 96090, Washington D.C. 20090-6090, who has the power to establish "special areas" that protect small natural recreation sites. You might be surprised how powerful your comments and requests can be.

8. LITTLE KACHESS LAKE

Features	▪ changing forest and lake
One way	▪ 1 mile or more
Elevation gain	▪ 250 feet
Difficulty	▪ easy to steep (wheelchair section)
Open	▪ summer
Maps	▪ Green Trails 208; campground brochure

First, an introduction to the forest here on an easy, gravel trail. Then, a rougher illustration of an old-fashioned trail of rocks and roots that struggles up and down above the lake toward destinations miles to the north.

Drive east on I-90 over Snoqualmie Pass, turning off at Exit 62 and turning left over the freeway to follow Forest Road 49 to the entrance of Kachess Campground in about 5 miles.

Beyond the entry station turn left at the T intersection and follow the campground road to the boat launch area, continuing left again around a parking loop to a spur right that leads to the trailhead parking area.

Little Kachess Lake

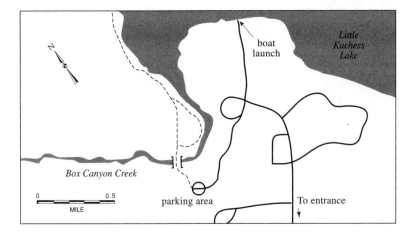

From the parking area take the trail past a display to a log bridge over Box Canyon Creek in less than 100 yards. Follow the barrier-free trail to the right to points overlooking the lake with displays that explain the full spectrum of nature here.

At the end of the loop, the paved path climbs to a bluff overlook with the fullest view of the lake and mountains across the way.

For a true sense of the ruggedness of these shores, proceed north beyond the end of the paved loop to the original lake trail. Here, the path, sometimes level and sometimes steep, skirts cliffs and bluffs or passes through old forest, seldom reaching the water's edge.

Go as far as the spirit moves you. In a little more than 4.5 miles, at the upper end of the lake, the trail reaches a junction with the Mineral Creek Trail, which leads into the Alpine Lakes Wilderness.

9. COOPER RIVER TRAIL

Features	▪	forest and wild river
One way	▪	3.25 miles
Elevation gain	▪	400 feet
Difficulty	▪	moderate to steep
Open	▪	summer
Map	▪	Green Trails 208

Two choices here: Walk generally downhill from Cooper Lake at 2,800 feet, or walk a shorter distance slightly uphill on the lower trail to view the pools not far from Salmon la Sac Campground at 2,400 feet.

Copper River

From I-90 turn off either at Exit 80 over the freeway to Bullfrog Road or at Exit 84 over the freeway to Cle Elum, driving in both instances to Highway 903, Roslyn, and beyond.

To hike down the river trail, drive about 18 miles north of Cle Elum on Highway 903, turning left on Forest Road 46 to cross the Cle Elum River and in 4.7 miles right on Spur Road 113. Find the trailhead downhill to the right in 0.2 mile, just beyond the bridge over the Cooper River.

To hike up the river trail from Salmon la Sac Campground, drive about 19 miles from Cle Elum to the end of paved Highway 903. Take the spur road to the right as you enter the campground, and find the trailhead in another 0.5 mile at the end of the road.

The trail down the river from Cooper Lake drops near the river through great old Douglas firs and hemlock to rock-slab views and fishing holes in 0.25 mile. The path then passes through more lush forest and more rock ledges, pools, and rapids before climbing away from the river to a cedar-guarded stream crossing—and a resting bench.

The trail now climbs up and down, sometimes out of earshot of the river, before dropping sharply back to spectacular views into a

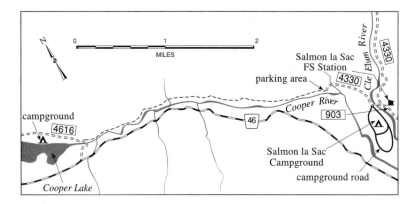

gorge of more torrents, pools, and rapids before finally reaching river level once again.

From the Salmon la Sac Campground, walk upstream past rapids, cliffs, and pools, picking the best place to stop, look, and listen to the stream. Walk about 0.25 mile farther up the trail, climbing about 200 feet, for a fuller vista down on the river.

10. TUCQUALA MEADOWS

Features	■	flower meadow
One way	■	as far as you like
Elevation gain	■	none
Difficulty	■	wet
Open	■	Memorial Day or later
Map	■	Green Trails 176

Too many flowers here to even attempt to identify—each at its own time and in its own season. But some of almost every flower at this elevation (3,400 feet) between the melting snows of spring and fall.

From I-90 take either Exit 80 over the freeway to Bullfrog Road or Exit 84 over the freeway to Cle Elum, driving in both instances to Highway 903, Roslyn, and beyond.

Drive to the end of paved Highway 903 in 19 miles from Cle Elum, bearing right up gravel Forest Road 4330 at a point where the paved road turns left to cross the river.

In another 10 miles find the meadow to the left just beyond Tucquala (Fish) Lake across from a guard station and Fish Lake Campground. (The meadow and trail-end of this sometimes rough road are blocked every spring by high water over the road at Scatter Creek. Check with the Cle Elum District Ranger Station about conditions before Memorial Day for sure.)

The meadow extends from the road to the Cle Elum River and from the primitive camp at the south to the forest at the north.

There are no trails in this meadow, nor should there be. This meadow is strictly for flowers, wild, unnamed, and unmarked, to be found wherever they grow in whatever time of summer you visit there.

Early in the spring, fields of blue-eyed grass are followed by larger fields of shooting stars. Later, columbines and tiger lilies, cotton grass and bog orchids, elephant's head and chocolate lilies (if you're there on time). And that only starts the list.

Bring rubber boots of some kind, for the meadows are soggy all summer long. Carry bug lotion if there is no wind. Take your flower book and camera for sure, and then wander where you will.

Leave all the flowers where you find them, naturally. If everyone who came this way took a flower home, there soon would be none left.

And, oh yes, explore the river's edge, watch for deer in the meadow, and sometimes, if you are lucky, glimpse across the stream—a bear.

Cathedral Rock from Tucquala Meadows

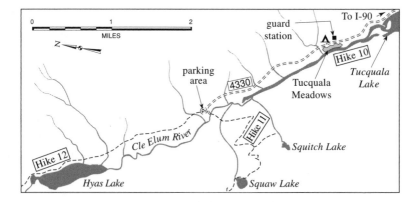

11. SQUAW LAKE

Features ■	lake and vistas
One way ■	2 miles
Elevation gain ■	1,450 feet
Difficulty ■	moderate to steep
Open ■	summer
Map ■	Green Trails 176

Big peaks and bigger lakes can't overawe this alpine gem. Walk slightly more than 2 miles from a beautiful valley to an equally beautiful lake surrounded by its own worthwhile peaks.

From I-90 turn off either at Exit 80 over the freeway to Bullfrog Road or at Exit 84 over the freeway to Cle Elum, driving in both instances to Highway 903, Roslyn, and beyond.

Drive to the end of paved Highway 903 in 19 miles, bearing right up gravel Forest Road 4330 at a point where the paved road turns left to cross the Cle Elum River. Find the trailhead in about 13 miles (almost at the end of Forest Road 4330) off a short spur road to the left. (See map above.) From the parking area, the trail crosses a bridge over the Cle Elum River into old forest in the Alpine Lakes Wilderness and then starts a 1,000-foot climb up long switchbacks to the top of a ridge and a junction with a trail down Trail Creek.

Turn right toward Cathedral Rock and climb more gradually now along the side of a ridge (views here over the valley) to the wooded, subalpine lake tucked in heather at 4,850 feet at the base of a rocky cliff. Piles of snow here last into the summer.

A worthy place to stop, with boulders to rest and lunch on. However, if the spirit moves you, walk on north toward Cathedral Rock into a series of meadows, rock outcrops, and patches of forest before turning back.

Squaw Lake

12. HYAS LAKE

Features	▪	lake below Cathedral Rock
One way	▪	2 miles or less
Elevation gain	▪	slight
Difficulty	▪	easy
Open	▪	summer
Map	▪	Green Trails 176

One of the easiest and most spectacular trips in this entire book.

From I-90 turn off either at Exit 80 over the freeway to Bullfrog Road or at Exit 84 over the freeway to Cle Elum, driving in both instances to Highway 903, Roslyn, and beyond.

Drive to the end of Highway 903 in about 19 miles, bearing right up gravel Road 4330 at a point where the paved road turns left to cross the Cle Elum River. Find the trailhead off the end of a parking area at the end of Forest Road 4330 in about 13 miles. (See map on page 42.)

The path wanders through an old-growth forest and along the edge of occasional meadows to a pretty lake nested below Cathedral Rock and Mount Daniel at 3,550 feet. Camp spots in timber just before the trail reaches the lake. Other camp spots along the lake.

The trail continues on to Little Hyas Lake in 0.25 mile and on to Deception Pass at 4,500 feet in another 2.5 miles. Views down on the lakes and up at the mountains from open slopes to the pass.

Much of the heavy wear on the trails here dates back to when the Pacific Crest Trail passed this way. Now the Crest Trail climbs across the ridge on the other side of the lake. You may spot hikers there.

Note: As the trail climbs from the parking lot, watch for ant hills, and, yes, ant "highways" at your feet alongside the trail. There is no saying exactly where they may be found. However, they are common in these dry forests and if you see one, take time to stop and admire their work and the steady hum from their busy "hill." And if near the trail, note the steady traffic on their much-traveled and well-maintained ant "highways" to who-knows-what hidden in the grass.

Hyas Lake

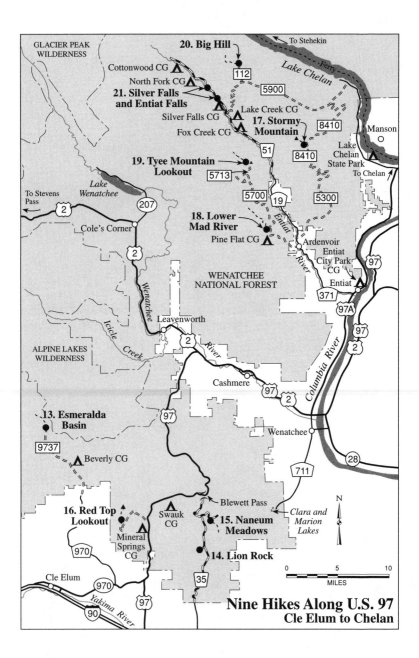

GLACIER PEAK
WILDERNESS

To Stehekin

20. Big Hill

Cottonwood CG

North Fork CG

Lake Chelan

112

5900

**21. Silver Falls
and Entiat Falls**

Silver Falls CG

Lake Creek CG

**17. Stormy
Mountain**

8410

Manson

Fox Creek CG

Lake
Chelan
State Park

8410

51

To Chelan

**19. Tyee Mountain
Lookout**

5713

5700

19

5300

To Stevens
Pass

Lake
Wenatchee

207

**18. Lower
Mad River**

Entiat

Pine Flat CG

2

Cole's Corner

Ardenvoir
Entiat
City Park
CG

Entiat

97

2

WENATCHEE
NATIONAL FOREST

371

97A

97

Wenatchee
River

Leavenworth

2

Columbia River

2

Icicle

Creek

ALPINE LAKES
WILDERNESS

97
Cashmere

2

**13. Esmeralda
Basin**

9737

Wenatchee

Beverly CG

711

28

N

Blewett Pass

Clara and
Marion
Lakes

**16. Red Top
Lookout**

Swauk
CG

**15. Naneum
Meadows**

Mineral
Springs
CG

970

14. Lion Rock

0   5   10

MILES

Cle Elum

970

35

Nine Hikes Along U.S. 97
Cle Elum to Chelan

97

90

Yakima River

Lookout on top of Red Mountain

CLE ELUM TO CHELAN

The Okanogan–Wenatchee National Forest east of the Cascades offers four distinct seasons in this dry country. You'll find green springs and colorful autumns here, hot summers in the valleys with cool winds in the higher Cascades, and snow at every elevation in the winter.

Find sweeping views of the mountains to the west and sprawling farmlands to the east from trails to two lookouts, **Red Top** (Hike 16) and **Tyee Mountain** (Hike 19). Big scenes, too, from **Big Hill** (Hike 20), **Stormy Mountain** (Hike 17), and **Lion Rock** (Hike 14). Two waterfalls on the **Entiat River** (Hike 21). With another waterfall and flower fields on the trail to **Esmeralda Basin** (Hike 13). Other trails follow creeks through meadows bordered by ancient lava ridges of basalt.

For information on campgrounds, see Appendix 1, Campgrounds. For the latest reports on trail and road conditions, telephone Cle Elum and Entiat Ranger Stations. See Appendix 2 for the Okanogan–Wenatchee National Forest website.

13. ESMERALDA BASIN

Features	■	high meadows and wildflowers
One way	■	2-plus miles
Elevation gain	■	1,200 feet
Difficulty	■	easy to steep
Open	■	midsummer
Map	■	Green Trails 209

Start with a rock-shredded waterfall and then hike into flower meadows that offer fresh bouquets for each new week in summer. And one weekly bouquet—truly—is no better than another.

Drive east on I-90 to Cle Elum and turn off at Exit 85 to Blewett Pass Highway 970/U.S. 97. In about 6 miles turn left onto Teanaway Road (later Forest Road 9737). Follow it to the end, about 22 miles from Highway 970. Find parking spots and picnic tables below the falls at the road's end.

The path starts to the right of the series of waterfalls (each short side trip to the river's edge brings a different view). Above the falls the path makes its way sharply upstream in a long 0.5 mile to a junction. Turn left at the fork with Lake Ingalls Trail.

Bear ahead now on an old mining road to an unmarked point in about 0.25 mile where the main trail turns to the right and climbs to a higher level on the slope and an older path proceeds ahead. Take either one. Or go up one and back the other, for both end at the head of the valley at about 5,200 feet.

Flowers here grow in all sorts of environments. Some bloom wildly

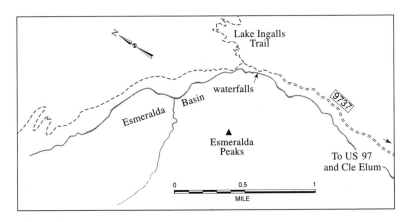

on bone-dry slopes. Others literally explode in marshy spots. Sometimes you'll find both, side by side.

The lower path makes its way on a soggy, unkept, and unmarked trail along the old road through a series of meadow pockets crowded with wet-rooted flowers.

The more developed upper path, just as interesting, climbs uphill through drier slopes and different flowers but with occasional soggy patches, too.

The trails join at the head of the valley in less than 2 miles in an open area where miners—and sometimes hikers—camp. Look up at diggings on the slopes. The path continues up the ridge to the right, leaving all the flowers behind.

Don't forget your flower book and camera, and, as you hike look up at the ridges for goats and, in the spring, for wilder waterfalls.

Elephanthead

14. LION ROCK

Features	■ high views
One way	■ as far as you like
Elevation gain	■ slight
Difficulty	■ unmarked but easy
Open	■ summer
Map	■ Green Trails 210

Stand on the rim of a massive ridge of basalt and look from 6,200 feet down into the Swauk Valley and out at Enchantment Peaks, Mount Stuart, and Mount Rainier—to the sound of coyotes in the gulches far below.

Drive east on I-90 to Cle Elum and turn off at Exit 85 onto Highway 970/U.S. 97 leading to Wenatchee. At Blewett (formerly Swauk) Pass, turn right onto Forest Road 9716, and in about 3 miles turn left onto Forest Road 9712 to a junction with Forest Road 35. Turn right (south) on Forest Road 35, driving another 4 miles to turn right again onto an unmarked spur road that leads past the small, primitive Lion Rock Spring Campground and spring, and on to a viewpoint from the old Lion Rock lookout site in another 0.75 mile.

As you travel Forest Road 35, much of it above 6,000 feet, stop at unmarked but obvious vista points on the west (right) side of the road. Wander here, too, if you wish. And be sure to note the stunted flowers that struggle on all of the ridges here.

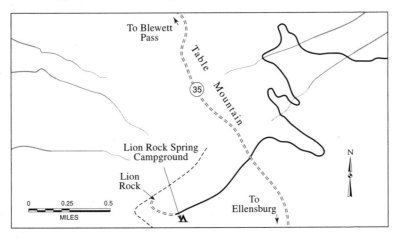

(For a more scenic but more complex route to Lion Rock with views over the Ellensburg countryside from every hairpin turn, take I-90 Exit 85 and follow Highway 970 to its junction with U.S. 97. Turn a hard right onto U.S. 97 and in 8 miles turn left onto Smithson Road. Drive east another 3.75 miles and turn left onto Forest Road 35, following it from about 2,000 feet to its paved and gravel end at more than 6,000 feet. Turn left to Lion Rock in another 0.25 mile. Open meadows and grander views the higher you drive.)

At Lion Rock, wander where you wish along the edge of the cliff. Jeep paths to the south. Pick your own way to the north through more flowers struggling to make it with little water in a so-short growing season.

You may find cattle joining you here. If you have to tent-camp and do not wish to share your tent with a curious cow, use the small fenced Lion Rock Springs Campground.

Mount Rainier from Lion Rock

15. NANEUM MEADOWS

Features	▪	high meadows, springs, basalt cliffs
One way	▪	1.5 miles
Elevation loss	▪	500 feet
Difficulty	▪	moderate to easy
Open	▪	summer
Map	▪	Green Trails 210

Only a small sample here of the high plateaus in the Wenatchee Mountains southwest of Wenatchee: meadows, flowers, bursts of basalt, springs, spurts of forest, and ancient ponderosa pines.

Drive east on I-90 to Cle Elum and turn off at Exit 85 onto Highway 970/U.S. 97 leading to Wenatchee. At Blewett (formerly Swauk) Pass, turn right onto Forest Road 9716, and in about 3 miles turn

Naneum Meadows

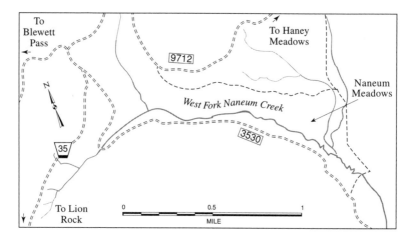

left onto Forest Road 9712. Pass the junction with Forest Road 35 and find the trailhead to the right downhill in little more than a mile.

(To be picked up at the lower end of the trail, have your driver return on Forest Road 9712, turning left on Forest Road 35 and left again in 0.5 mile onto Forest Road 3530. Find the exit of the trailhead in about 2 miles, downhill on the left.)

The trail starts at the top through sage and lupine meadows at 5,600 feet and drops shortly into forest and around a spring fenced for cattle. Keep right here but generally proceed straight ahead as the trail grows faint, picking up blazes on trees beyond the clearing.

Note the snags of great old ponderosa pines and Douglas fir as the path joins a wider trail from the left before dropping to Naneum Creek and Trail 1381.

As you drop downhill, note the dusting places for cows and elk beneath the trees and wonder what a rusty old truck bumper is doing near the trail.

At the bottom take the heaviest-traveled trail to the right. Places for no-fire camping here on unsigned spurs that lead into coves surrounded by mounds of basalt.

The path crosses Naneum Creek and makes its way past more ridges of basalt on one side and verdant meadows on the other.

You can see the road across the way now, so take time to wander the meadows before returning to the trail, turning right across a bridge and walking back into forest to the highway trailhead at about 5,100 feet.

The best time to walk here is early in summer, before cattle eat the flowers and muck up the paths.

16. RED TOP LOOKOUT

Features	■	agate fields and vistas
One way	■	1 mile or less
Elevation gain	■	360 feet or less
Difficulty	■	moderate to very steep
Open	■	summer
Maps	■	Green Trails 209, 210

Hike to the lookout tower at 5,361 feet for views to be seen no place else in this area and then, on a lower trail, to an agate field that looks more like an artillery or missile target range than a meadow.

Drive east on I-90 to Cle Elum and take Exit 85 onto Highway 970/U.S. 97 leading to Wenatchee. In 18 miles beyond Cle Elum, turn left off U.S. 97 (about 0.1 mile beyond Mineral Springs Campground) onto Forest Road 9738. In 2.6 miles turn left on Forest Road 9702, driving 5 miles more to the parking and picnic area.

Find the trail to both the lookout and the agate fields off a road loop above the parking area.

To reach the lookout, turn uphill to the left at a trail junction in about 25 yards from the road onto a trail that climbs steeply and persistently to the lookout in, as the sign says, 1 mile, although it may be less and seem more.

As you near the top, note the desert flowers that manage to grow in the rock scree surrounding the tower. But don't disturb any of the plants you see. Admire them, yes, but consider the struggle they made to gain a foothold in this barren, unstable slope and leave them for others to admire.

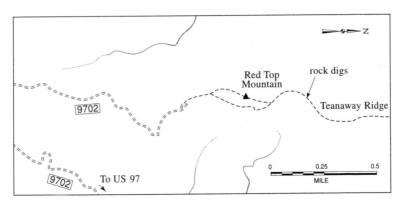

Agate beds near Red Top Lookout

From the tower—on a clear day—see Rainier, Stuart, the tip of Adams, and the other peaks in the Cascades as well as the Ellensburg and Cle Elum valleys. Carry an Okanogan–Wenatchee National Forest map to identify most of the nearby peaks you see.

To visit the agate beds—and you really should—either continue on the ridge north of the lookout or, at the start, turn right at the junction off the parking area.

The lookout trail drops to the agate fields and loops back to the parking area. The trail from the parking area stays below the ridge with vistas to the east as it climbs to a meadow, and then immediately to the target-range agate beds. Spur trails to the east lead into the maze of uncovered holes dug and re-dug by rockhounds searching for agates and thunderstones, which are, apparently, after decades of digging, still being sought and found. If you're not an expert on these stones, talk to diggers and they'll show you what they're looking for.

There's a kind of frenzy demonstrated here for sure. Yet, as you'll note, the poor trees still survive. A teepee-shaped outhouse erected by a rockhound group stands in the middle of the carnage.

17. STORMY MOUNTAIN

Features ▪	spectacular vistas from 7,200 feet
One way ▪	1.5 miles
Elevation gain ▪	1,100 feet
Difficulty ▪	steep
Open ▪	summer
Map ▪	Green Trails 147

Hike to a former lookout site with views that stretch from the wheat fields of eastern Washington, over the apple orchards of Chelan, to the Cascades as far south (on a clear day) as Mount Adams with the maw of Mount St. Helens and Glacier Peak thrown in.

Drive east on I-90 to Cle Elum and turn off at Exit 85 onto Highway 970/U.S. 97 leading to Wenatchee. From Wenatchee drive north to either Entiat or Lake Chelan State Park, the simplest route being from Lake Chelan.

From Lake Chelan State Park, drive up the lake to Twentyfive Mile Creek, turning uphill onto Forest Road 5900 and then left in 2.5 miles onto Forest Road 8410. Views out over Lake Chelan, Chelan, Manson, and the Columbia Basin in about 8 miles, reaching the trailhead at a saddle atop the Chelan Mountain ridge, 20 miles from the lake.

From Entiat, drive 10 miles east to Ardenvoir, turning right in another 1.4 miles onto Mud Creek Road 5300 and then left in 5.9 miles more onto Forest Road 8410, signed "Baldy Mountain." In about

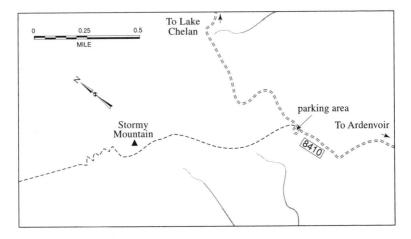

4 more miles, the road climbs past a maze of unmarked, often confusing, junctions before contouring around Baldy Mountain and climbing on to the trailhead at a saddle atop the ridge, about 21 miles from Ardenvoir. (There's less confusion coming down.)

From a parking area at the saddle, the trail climbs to the west a steep 0.75 mile leveling off in another 0.75 mile just below the summit. At the highest point on the trail take a spur path to the right through silver stumps to the old lookout site with lots of places to wander and miles and miles to see.

One sad note, though: As the trailhead sign says, the trail is an example of "your ORV dollars at work," or more truly, an example of how the public's auto gas tax "hiker" money is being used to reconstruct a "road" for motorcycles that are already grinding ruts in the path you paid for. Many of the trails in this forest district are open to use by motorcycles.

Weather-bleached trees on top of Stormy Mountain

18. LOWER MAD RIVER

Features	■	forest along a river trail
One way	■	1.5 miles or less
Elevation gain	■	slight
Difficulty	■	easy
Open	■	summer
Map	■	Green Trails 147

An easy and pleasant walk up a shady river canyon from Pine Flat Campground on the Mad River.

Drive east on I-90 to Cle Elum and turn off at Exit 85 onto Highway 970/U.S. 97 leading to Wenatchee. From the junction of U.S. 2 and 97 just west of Wenatchee, drive north on U.S. 97A to Entiat in 15 miles. At Entiat turn left to Ardenvoir, another 10 miles.

Lower Mad River

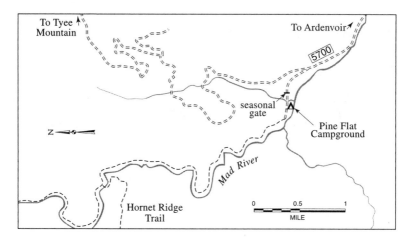

A short 0.5 mile beyond Ardenvoir turn left onto Forest Road 5700, driving about 3 miles to a steep spur road on the left that drops down to the campground (sometimes not signed).

The trail off the uphill end of the campground follows the twisting river to Hornet Creek and beyond. Most pleasant the first mile.

Note in this valley how older trees with their thick bark were badly scorched but not destroyed by the ground fires that raged through here sometime in the past. Watch, too, for groves of trees that beavers once envisioned using for a dam. Some trees you'll see were gnawed but never felled before the dam builders abandoned whatever plans they had. Find the junction with Hornet Ridge Trail across the river to the left in 1.5 miles. And watch for rattlesnakes on the trail all along the way.

19. TYEE MOUNTAIN LOOKOUT

Features	■	vistas and meadows from 6,600 feet
One way	■	as far as you wish to go
Elevation gain	■	slight
Difficulty	■	moderate, steep in spots
Open	■	midsummer
Map	■	Green Trails 147

Less than two decades ago, this lookout was best known for its view of the damage wrought by wildfires that swept across all the ridges seen from here.

Tyee Ridge Trail

Today, the lookout looks out on greenery once again. Most of the burned snags have fallen or turned to silver ghosts, and the mountainsides and panoramas are again worthy of your time. The lookout is staffed some years when the fire danger is high.

Drive east on I-90 to Cle Elum and turn off at Exit 85 onto Highway 970/U.S. 97 leading to Wenatchee. From the junction of U.S. 2 and 97 just west of Wenatchee, drive north on U.S. 97A to Entiat in 15 miles. Turn left to Ardenvoir in another 10 miles.

In a short 0.5 mile beyond Ardenvoir, turn left onto Forest Road 5700, driving about 15 miles before turning right uphill to Spur Road

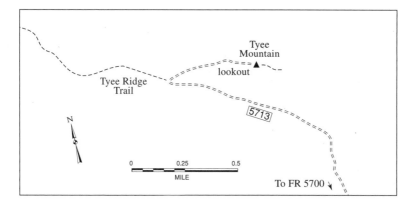

5713. Continue another 4.2 miles over a rougher road to the lookout site. (Logging some years may disrupt signing.)

From the lookout, a circle of mountains here: Stuart, Rainier, Adams, Glacier Peak, and all the Cascades and the North Cascades.

But don't stop your vista-gawking at the tower. Park at the switchback just below the tower and hike west out Tyee Ridge Trail.

First, stand there in awe of the ghost forest created by the furnace of flame that consumed this ridge. Then note that not every tree was destroyed in the holocaust. The few that survive live now to reseed the slope. And finally, note how the birds have returned. And the flowers. And the tracks of deer and scat of smaller animals.

The trail continues more than 5 miles along the ridge. Walk as far as the scene informs and pleases you.

20. BIG HILL

Features	▪	panoramas, old burn, forest, meadows
One way	▪	2 miles
Elevation gain	▪	400 feet
Difficulty	▪	steep
Open	▪	midsummer
Maps	▪	Green Trails 114, 115, 146, 147; Okanogan–Wenatchee National Forest map

Big views, as you'd expect, from a former lookout site. But special views from a trail that crosses an old burn, climbs into old, untouched forest, and rests in high meadows.

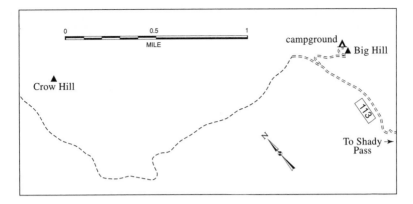

The fire here, started by lightning in August 1970, swept the entire Silver Creek basin before being stopped by firefighters at the top of the ridge.

Drive east on I-90 to Cle Elum and turn off at Exit 85 onto Highway 970/U.S. 97 leading to Wenatchee. From the junction of U.S. 2 and 97 just west of Wenatchee, drive north on U.S. 97A toward Entiat and turn left in 15 miles to Ardenvoir/Entiat River Road 51. Turn right in 29 miles (beyond Lake Creek Campground) to Forest Road 5900, following it to Shady Pass (vista there) in about 8.5 miles. At the pass, turn left on Forest Road 112 and drive about 2 miles (still more views here) to a point where Forest Road 112 turns sharply uphill to the right and Forest Road 113 continues to the trailhead.

Drive or walk the steep Forest Road 112 less than 0.25 mile uphill to top of Big Hill (6,827 feet), the former lookout site, and primitive camp and cabin with mementos of the fire. The 360-degree views here include everything from Glacier Peak past Lake Chelan around to Mount Rainier and back again.

Once satisfied, return to Forest Road 113 and the trail. The path, off the left side of the road-end, drops down a fire line to a saddle, becoming a formal trail as it climbs from the left of the saddle through a burned forest. Note as you walk here how one tree or clump of trees, all white skeletons now, was burned while another was not as the fire swept up the slope to stop at the fire line along the crest of the Chelan ridge. Note, too, how the flowers are returning and the lodgepole (always first to appear) and white pines are establishing themselves again.

The trail soon climbs gracefully up to another saddle at nearly 7,000 feet and immediately enters a forest untouched by fire. Take time here to cross a meadow to look beyond Lake Chelan.

Pyramid Mountain from Big Hill Trail

91. SILVER FALLS AND ENTIAT FALLS

Features	▪	the best of waterfalls
One way	▪	0.5 mile to Silver Falls
Elevation gain	▪	600 feet to Silver Falls
Difficulty	▪	easy at Entiat but steep at Silver Falls
Open	▪	summer
Map	▪	Green Trails 146

Two spectacular waterfalls: one you can almost stand under but have to work to get to, and another you can sit beside by simply wandering to it. Both near campgrounds and within about 2.5 miles of each other.

Drive east on I-90 to Cle Elum and turn off at Exit 85 onto Highway 970/U.S. 97 leading to Wenatchee. From the junction of U.S. 2 and 97 just west of Wenatchee, drive north on U.S. 97A toward Entiat and turn left in 15 miles to Ardenvoir/Entiat River Road 51. Reach Silver Falls in 30 miles; Entiat Falls in 32.5 miles.

Silver Falls. Find the nature trail to the series of Silver Falls on the north side of the road across from a parking area and display board at the entrance of Silver Falls Campground.

At the first fork in the trail with its formal viewing platform, turn right on a path that drops over a footbridge and then zigzags up along the tumbling creek.

Four more viewpoints offer different perspectives of the series of falls as you climb. At the first ledge go straight ahead to a cooling seat. Return to the trail and continue uphill to yet another perspective and another place to rest.

Reach the third and best viewpoint by climbing higher, still below towering slabs of rock, to a point almost underneath the falls. How-

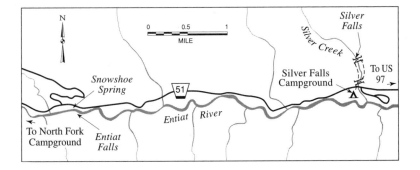

ever, don't try to stand beneath the dripping cliff. The wet rocks are very slippery. Views here out over the valley, too.

The last and longest spurt of trail switchbacks up and away from the creek before returning to a bridge over a small sliding waterfall. Then drop back to the first trail junction past more views over the valley and one more perspective of the falls.

Entiat Falls. Find the trail to Entiat Falls on the Entiat River to the left of the road off a parking strip. Here the path drops to a pool below the falls. In early summer watch for water ouzels (dippers) feeding chicks in niches of rock bordering the falls. Look for yellow mouths gaping from almost-hidden nest holes in dripping moss. Also reach the falls by trail from North Fork Campground.

Silver Falls

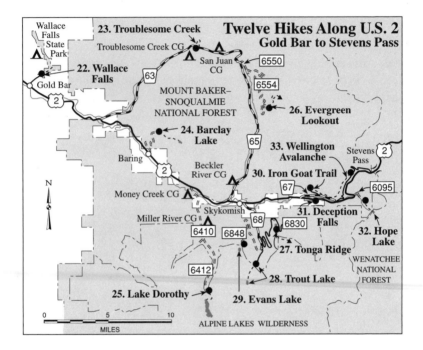

Twelve Hikes Along U.S. 2
Gold Bar to Stevens Pass

Wallace Falls State Park

22. Wallace Falls

Gold Bar

23. Troublesome Creek

Troublesome Creek CG

San Juan CG

6550

6554

26. Evergreen Lookout

63

MOUNT BAKER–SNOQUALMIE NATIONAL FOREST

24. Barclay Lake

Baring

65

33. Wellington Avalanche

Stevens Pass

2

Beckler River CG

30. Iron Goat Trail

Money Creek CG

67

6095

31. Deception Falls

Skykomish

Miller River CG

68

32. Hope Lake

6410

6848

6830

27. Tonga Ridge

WENATCHEE NATIONAL FOREST

6412

28. Trout Lake

N

25. Lake Dorothy

29. Evans Lake

0   5   10

MILES

ALPINE LAKES WILDERNESS

Lake Dorothy

TWELVE HIKES ALONG U.S. 2

GOLD BAR TO STEVENS PASS

There's beauty here and tragic history mixed with lakes, lookouts, and exciting trails.

One trail with two entrances defines the tragic history of a railroad in **Iron Goat Trail** (Hike 30 and Hike 33) at Stevens Pass. A short and easy loop path on noisy **Troublesome Creek** (Hike 23) offers everything a mountain creek could possibly display. **Wallace Falls** (Hike 22) roars past viewpoint after viewpoint. **Evergreen Lookout** (Hike 26) provides the highest views. Three lakes display their beauties in three differing mountain settings.

For information on campgrounds nearby, see Appendix 1, Campgrounds. For last minute reports on trail and road conditions telephone the Washington State Park Information office, the Skykomish Ranger District, or see the Mount Baker–Snoqualmie National Forest website (see Appendix 2).

22. WALLACE FALLS

Features ▪	waterfall
One way ▪	2 miles or more
Elevation gain ▪	up to 1,100 feet
Difficulty ▪	moderate to steep
Open ▪	all year
Map ▪	Green Trails 142

You can glimpse this waterfall high in the mountains to the left of U.S. 2 as you drive to Gold Bar. But with a little effort, you can feel its cold spray, too. One of the most popular, accessible, and spectacular waterfalls in the region.

Drive east on the U.S. 2 through Monroe to Gold Bar, following signs to the left 2 miles to Wallace Falls State Park. The trail to the falls is clearly marked at the end of the limited parking area, which may be filled on summer weekends.

The path starts out (at 600 feet) below an unexciting powerline and turns shortly into a dense, second-growth forest before reaching a fork in another 100 yards.

By continuing left on the railroad grade, it's 2 miles on a still slow-climbing and uneventful path to where the two trails join again. Or, by dropping downhill to the right, it's a shorter but steeper mile, crossing a wooden bridge and then climbing generally through a dense forest of hemlock and Douglas fir amid alders and vine maples, ferns, and forest wildflowers in season.

From the juncture of both trails, walk another 0.25 mile to a picnic

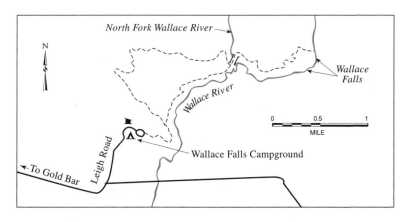

Wallace Falls

shelter (870 feet) and views up at the falls. Or climb ahead to a middle viewpoint (1,120 feet), or still farther to a view of the valley (1,400 feet), or still farther in 3 miles (1,700 feet) to an explosive vista of everything: down on the falls, out over the valley, across at the mountains on the other side, and out on the string of villages along the river. Each and every point is worth the effort.

With one reminder: Rocks constantly washed with spray from the falls are always slippery. So be advised. Don't venture from the trails to get a "better look." At anything. Some have slipped with fatal results. Remain safely on the trail!

23. TROUBLESOME CREEK

Features	■	grand forest plus a wild stream
One way	■	0.5-mile loop
Elevation gain	■	slight
Difficulty	■	moderate
Open	■	summer
Map	■	Green Trails 143

What was once an old miners' trail is now a busy, pretty, and popular interpretive trail along and around a tumbling, noisy creek. It's also a trail to be savored and enjoyed because what you see here is a sample of all that's the best in flowers, trees, and turbulent streams to be seen anywhere.

Troublesome Creek

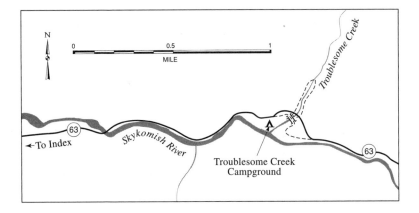

Drive east on U.S. 2 through Gold Bar, turning left in about 8 miles toward Index on North Fork Road 63. Turn right in about 11 miles into the Troublesome Creek Campground entrance. Take a stub road immediately to the left, and park near a footbridge over Troublesome Creek. Don't cross the footbridge. Find your path up the left side of the creek. (You'll return to the far side of the bridge at the end of your walk.)

The path dips under the highway bridge and proceeds upstream above a very noisy creek through a towering old forest of Douglas fir and cedar trees.

The path climbs to a viewpoint over a roaring gorge where water races one way and then turns and plunges another, all the while sculpting bowls and sweeping curves in shoreside rock.

Beyond the view and resting point, the trail wanders through a forest of monstrous boulders to a bridge where the stream again displays the essence of its violence. An undeveloped upriver path on the far side of the bridge crosses inviting slabs and eroded folds of rock near an ancient cedar still clinging to its perch on the very edges of the stream.

The main path turns right on the far side of the bridge to climb past more old giants surrounded by fallen, rotting snags of failed competitors, more forest flowers, plus the sounds of birds, squirrels, and chipmunks above the noise of the creek.

At the base of a giant Douglas fir on this part of the trail, pause for a moment on a bench and rejoice that such forests can still be seen, heard, smelled, touched, and, if huckleberries are in fruit, tasted, too.

When you see the road, follow switchbacks down to the river, crossing beneath the road and over the wooden bridge to your car.

24. BARCLAY LAKE

Features	■	forest and lake
One way	■	1.5 miles
Elevation gain	■	100 feet
Difficulty	■	moderate
Open	■	summer
Map	■	Green Trails 143

Walk out of a recovering clear-cut into a rich forest and then on to a lake at 2,300 feet with places to sit and dream in the shadow of spectacular Baring Mountain.

Drive east on U.S. 2 from Monroe through Gold Bar, past the Index junction, and in another 6 miles to the village of Baring, turning left across the railroad tracks as you reach the store on the right. Across the railroad tracks proceed straight ahead, bearing left on Forest Road 6024 at the edge of town. Trailhead at the end of the road in about 4.5 miles.

The trail starts up an old fire line, turning right to the unmarked main trail in about 0.25 mile. The path then enters a forest that appears to be in a state of terminal collapse. Yet everywhere around you is a classic example of an old-growth forest, evolving still with broken snags filled with woodpecker holes, snarls of fallen rotting trees, and a ground littered with what seems like wasted debris. But all of it below a forest of old-growth giants towering above younger trees that wait

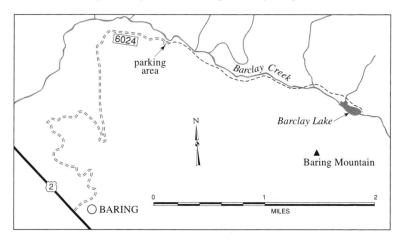

in the shade for their time and place in the sun, themselves towering over new seedlings creeping out of a mossy forest floor.

And take a second look at the forest floor: held intact by both old and living roots, protected by a sponge of duff and moss, awash with huckleberries, salmonberries, fireweed, and flowers of the shade.

The trail crosses Barclay Creek shortly before reaching the lake below the towering walls of Baring Mountain. The path proceeds the full length of the shore with your choice of camp, picnic, and viewing spots. Busy on weekends, however.

Barclay Lake below Baring Mountain

25. LAKE DOROTHY

Features	■	large mountain lake
One way	■	2 miles
Elevation gain	■	800 feet
Difficulty	■	moderate to steep
Open	■	summer
Map	■	Green Trails 175

The biggest alpine lake and one of the most beautiful on the west side of the Cascade Crest—with waterfalls en route.

Drive east on U.S. 2 about 11 miles beyond Index, turning right, just before you reach the tunnel west of Skykomish, to the old Cascade Highway and Money Creek Campground. In a little more than a mile, turn right again onto Miller River Road 6412 and drive to trailhead parking at the end.

Take at least two snacks on this walk. Eat the first at the footbridge over Camp Robber Creek (water ouzels but no camp robbers here). Save the rest for the final steep pitch to the log-jammed outlet of the lake at 3,000 feet.

The trail continues along the east side of the 2-mile-long, island-dotted lake, turning westward across the marshy far end before climbing on to more distant Bear, Deer, and Snoqualmie Lakes. One problem here: It is a challenge to catch the beauty of this place in a single camera shot. There are islands here. Floating driftwood in ever-changing shapes. Grand trees. Flowers. Mountains looming everywhere. Take a lot of film.

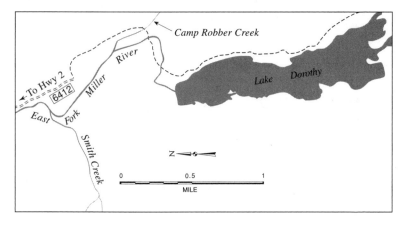

Lake Dorothy

26. EVERGREEN LOOKOUT

Features	■	spectacular vistas and high meadow
One way	■	1.5 miles
Elevation gain	■	1,300 feet
Difficulty	■	steep to very steep
Open	■	midsummer
Map	■	Green Trails 143
Note	■	check road access before leaving home

To be or not to be. That was the question here. As Shakespeare might have said, 'twas once, yet is still a lovely place.

The lookout, the colorful flower meadows, and grand views still survive. Even the road remains. So too the trail that leads from the end of the road and makes its way uphill sharply through a clear-cut and across a burned ridge to high views of everywhere.

For awhile, the Forest Service considered abandoning the lookout after a bridge washed out the narrow road leading to the lookout

Monte Cristo Peaks from Evergreen Mountain

trailhead. For several years it required an extra 8-mile walk up the logging road before you could even start your climb. In the eyes of some, it seemed then, repair of the bridge and logging road would cost too much. There was talk of building a new trail or converting the logging road into a trail.

In the end, the Forest Service fixed the bridge and decided to keep the 8-mile dirt road open to the trailhead from August to October, gating the road in the summer to protect nesting spotted owls. Best of all, the agency now offers hikers the privilege of renting the lookout on a nightly basis.

With the repair of the washout and opening of the road, the trail to the lookout again leads 1.5 miles sharply up the mountain. All of the flower meadows and distant mountains remain to be enjoyed. And hikers have an opportunity to soak up the beauty at their leisure.

So, after making your reservation, drive east on U.S. 2 from Everett

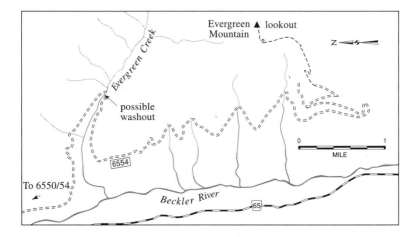

or Monroe to Skykomish, turn north on the Beckler River Road 65 and drive 12.5 miles to Jack Pass and Forest Road 6550/54. Turn right and follow 6554 as it winds over the slide area at Evergreen Creek and zigzags back and forth 8 miles to the trailhead at 4,300 feet. And there let the spectacular views return!

27. TONGA RIDGE

Features ■	forest, meadows, vistas
One way ■	2 miles, more or less
Elevation gain ■	up to 300 feet
Difficulty ■	moderate
Open ■	summer
Maps ■	Green Trails 175, 176

In less than 2 miles, climb a forested ridge to grass meadows at 4,600 to 4,800 feet along Tonga Ridge with views of Glacier Peak south through the glaciers of Mount Hinman. Lots of huckleberries in the fall.

Drive east on U.S. 2 from Everett or Monroe to Skykomish, turning south (right) on Foss River Road 68, about 0.5 mile east of the Skykomish District Ranger Station. In 3.7 miles turn left uphill on Forest Road 6830, driving another 6.8 miles to Spur Road 310 uphill to the right. Trailhead at the end of the spur road in less than 1.5 miles.

(Continue on Forest Road 6830 to views of the valley and mountains to the north. Take your Mount Baker–Snoqualmie forest map to identify all the peaks.)

Tonga Ridge Trail

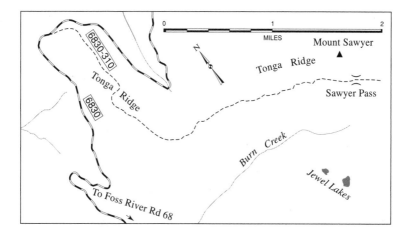

The trail, off the end of a parking area, starts out on the edge of a fire lane of an old clear-cut and shortly enters the Alpine Lakes Wilderness with its changing forest of silver fir, hemlock, and alpine fir. Open meadows in about 1.5 miles. Watch for a spur trail to the left here that leads to several viewpoints on the ridge. View here over the Skykomish valley and mountains to the north.

The main trail drops slightly then climbs again to more open meadows on the south slope of the ridge. Again, take spur trails to the ridge top for the best in vistas.

Ample places to pause and enjoy amid lots of lupine and humming-birds anxious to check out anything that's red.

28. TROUT LAKE

Features	▪	lake, forest, rockfalls
One way	▪	1.5 miles
Elevation gain	▪	400 feet
Difficulty	▪	moderate
Open	▪	summer
Map	▪	Green Trails 175

Hike through groves of grand old Douglas fir, past huge boulders that have tumbled from cliffs above you, over an avalanche of rocks to an interesting and pleasant mountain lake at 2,000-plus feet.

Drive east on U.S. 2 past Skykomish, turning south (right) on Foss River Road 68 about 0.5 mile east of the Skykomish District

Trout Lake

Ranger Station. Follow Forest Road 68 as it jogs to the left in about 5 miles and continues to trailhead parking at the end of the road.

The heavily used trail starts at the end of the parking area and enters the Alpine Lakes Wilderness in 100 yards or so, crossing a gravel bar to a log bridge over the Foss River in about 0.5 mile.

The trail travels through groves of hemlock and Douglas fir and past an array of giant boulders, which over centuries have tumbled off the pinnacles rimming the valley, hinting at rockfalls yet to come.

In about 1 mile, the path pauses at a giant Douglas fir and then climbs to views back on it as it towers alone, king of the forest here. As the trail turns back into the forest, note pipes exposed across the trail—remnants of a failed mining operation.

The path drops to the river again and crosses a 1991 avalanche track where a massive mound of rock plunged more than 1,000 feet from cliffs on Malachite Peak (to your right) burying the original trail. A thunderstorm appeared to have triggered the avalanche.

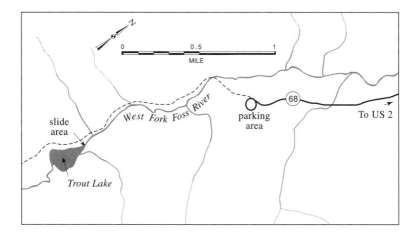

The dead trees near the water's edge were drowned when the lake, dammed by the rock, rose 7 feet. The water has since receded.

Find camping and resting spots along the shore. The trail continues along the lake before climbing almost 2,000 feet more to still other lakes.

29. EVANS LAKE

Features	▪	small and pleasant mountain lake
One way	▪	0.5 mile
Elevation gain	▪	slight
Difficulty	▪	easy
Open	▪	summer
Map	▪	Green Trails 175

A short path through rich forest leads to a pretty, wooded lake just inside the Alpine Lakes Wilderness.

Drive east on U.S. 2 past Skykomish, turning south (right) on Foss River Road 68 about 0.5 mile east of the Skykomish District Ranger Station. In about 5 miles, as Forest Road 68 jogs to the left to Trout Lake, continue ahead on Forest Road 6840 (views over the valley as you climb), turning right on Forest Road 6846 in about 4 miles and driving another 2.5 miles to the trailhead (keep left at the 2-mile marker). The trail is signed uphill on the right across from a parking area, just before the road crosses the bridge over the Evans Lake outlet creek.

Evans Lake

The path climbs gently through heather along the creek in open, lush forest, arriving suddenly at the lake. The path continues around the lake to the right, past a couple of camp spots at the upper end.

A peaceful place. What more to say?

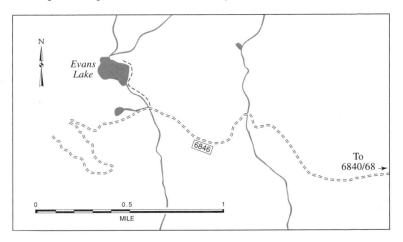

30. IRON GOAT TRAIL

Features	■	history plus scenery
One way	■	2 miles or more
Elevation gain	■	about 200 feet
Difficulty	■	easy to moderate (some wheelchair access)
Open	■	summer
Map	■	ask for brochure at the Forest Service ranger station in Skykomish

Walk an easy wheelchair trail through railroad history or climb spur trails to a hiker-only path on a higher section of the old Great Northern railroad grade with more history still.

And the mystery here? How trains were able to change direction without going around a curve. They simply backed up.

Wall No. 1 (the waterfall wall) was part of a former snowshed

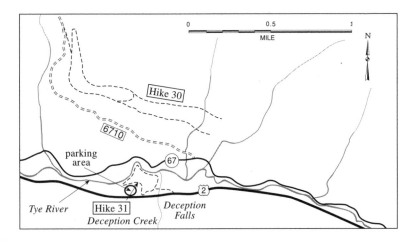

Drive east on U.S. 2 through Skykomish, turning north (left) at milepost 55 onto paved but unsigned Forest Road 67. (If you miss that turn, continue another 3.5 miles toward Scenic, turning left onto the other end of the same Forest Road 67.)

Continue from either end of Forest Road 67 to Forest Road 6710, uphill to the north, finding the trailhead in about 1.5 miles. Parking area along the road.

The well-developed wheelchair path starts through an alder grove filled with berry bushes and ferns and continues little more than a mile down the lower section of the railway right-of-way past viewpoints to a tunnel portal at a washed out creek. (Footpaths on this lower stretch of trail will eventually drop to Scenic on U.S. 2.)

A hiker trail leads uphill in the first 0.5 mile of the lower trail to a higher switchback level on the old railroad bed, which includes other collapsed tunnels and snow sheds. A second trail drops down to form a 1.5-mile loop. Or continue east on the upper level to a viewpoint beyond a collapsed flume in about 2 miles, returning to the trailhead in a total of 5.5 miles.

The upper trail ends at the old townsite of Wellington, destroyed along with a passenger train in an avalanche in which ninety-six passengers were killed. (See Hike 33, Wellington Avalanche).

These trails are all within the Stevens Pass Historic District, which extends over Stevens Pass and includes Deception Falls (Hike 31), Wellington Avalanche (Hike 33), and Bygone Byways (Hike 35). So how did the trains go around corners by backing up? With engines both front and back—coming or going—engineers drove into a spur from one track, stopped and then backed up onto another track going in the other direction, repeating the act several times as the train went up or down a mountain.

31. DECEPTION FALLS

Features	■	wild waterfalls in rich forest
One way	■	0.75-mile loop
Elevation gain	■	less than 200 feet
Difficulty	■	easy to moderate (wheelchair access)
Open	■	spring to fall
Map	■	Green Trails 176

Come face to face with a raging torrent and then walk through a peaceful forest to lesser tumults on a creek fed by a half-dozen or more lakes in the Alpine Lakes Wilderness.

Deception Falls

Drive east on U.S. 2 about 8 miles beyond Skykomish to a signed parking area on the north (left) side of the highway. (See map on page 84.)

The path starts to the left of a picnic shelter, dropping downhill to the right on a wheelchair portion of the path leading across a bridge over the creek to a platform beneath the highway, with a spectacular and noisy head-on view of the falls only feet away.

Return to the loop trail and drop downhill to the right across a log bridge to a quieter part of the creek in ancient, rainforest-like groves and then on to an overlook of another falls that tumbles into a pretty pool filled with rainbows if the sun is just right.

The path passes still more pools and then another small falls, sometimes snagged with logs thrown up on rocks during high water in the spring, reaching a more subdued section of stream where falls turn into rapids before climbing back to a picnic shelter.

As you climb toward the highway, note the great stumps of trees logged by hand by men who stood on springboards jammed into notches in trees to hand-saw the trees.

Display boards describe natural features along the way.

The falls development is within the Stevens Pass Historic District.

32. HOPE LAKE

Features ■	alpine lake and meadows
One way ■	about 1.5 miles
Elevation gain ■	1,300 feet
Difficulty ■	steep to very steep
Open ■	midsummer
Map ■	Green Trails 176

You don't have to walk far, but you do have to climb persistently to a pretty little mountain lake tucked into the very crest of the Cascades at 4,400 feet.

Drive 12 miles east of Skykomish on U.S. 2, turning right onto Forest Road 6095 a little more than 1 mile beyond the railroad overpass at Scenic and just before the highway widens to four lanes on a sharp highway turn. From Forest Road 6095, turn right in 0.6 mile onto Spur Road 110. Continue straight ahead at the next junction in 0.8 mile, turning right in 1.2 miles onto Spur Road 112. Spur Road 112 climbs steeply 1.3 miles to the trailhead at 3,000 feet.

The path, much of it built and maintained by The Mountaineers

Hope Lake

Singles, starts out in forest and then settles down to a steady climb above Tunnel Creek, reaching a saddle and the small lake (in Chelan County) on the Pacific Crest Trail at 4,400 feet.

But don't hurry away. If you've got time—and you should plan to take it—walk either north or south (or both) on the Pacific Crest Trail, exploring other meadows and heathered tarns.

The trail north toward Stevens Pass climbs over the divide to Mig Lake (4,600 feet, in King County) in about 0.75 mile. The path to the south climbs past unnamed tarns before climbing higher on the ridge.

And, finally, after soaking up all scenery right and left, promise to return again.

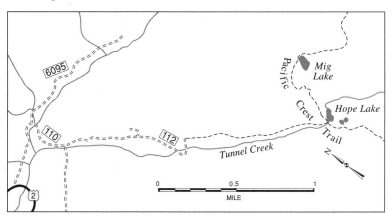

33. WELLINGTON AVALANCHE

Features ▪ a history—ninety-six people killed
One way ▪ as far as you like
Elevation gain ▪ slight
Difficulty ▪ easy
Open ▪ summer
Maps ▪ Green Trails 144, 176

It seems impossible standing amongst the trees and wildflowers on this mountain shelf today, but ninety-six people were killed here in March 1910 when a single wild spring avalanche swept two side-by-side railroad trains off their tracks into the roaring Tye River below.

To visit this historic site from Seattle (see Hike 30, Iron Goat Trail and Hike 31, Deception Falls, all part of the Stevens Pass Historical District) drive to the top of Stevens Pass and then loop back east (below the crest) turning right onto the Old Cascade Highway in a quarter mile. In 0.5 mile turn right again onto a gravel spur that ends in 0.1 mile at a parking and display area. From the east, crest Stevens Pass and drive down quickly to the Old Cascade Highway on the right.

The 3-mile tunnel through the mountains to the east and the snow sheds along the abandoned railway to the west are all that

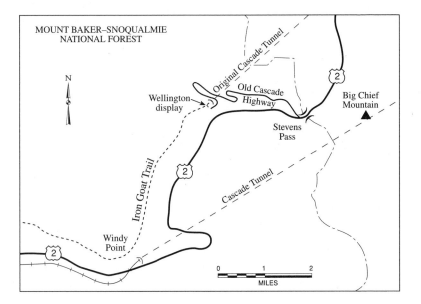

Wellington Tunnel

remain of Wellington, now a scenic history stop still at an altitude of 3,100 feet.

In 1910, heavy snow from a violent storm blocked the zigzag rail tracks that led from the tunnel down to Scenic, the railroad town now at the mouth of a lower tunnel still in use. The two trains could not be moved, and passengers decided to spend the night on the train while rotary plows continued attempts to clear the track.

That night while they slept a heavy rain and thunderstorm softened the snow and at 1:30 in the morning of March 1, a half-mile slab of heavy snow broke away from a mountain. The powerful avalanche missed the Wellington station and slammed into the side-by-side trains, parked where today's concrete snow shed is, knocking the cars and engines off their tracks and pitching them over the ledge straight down into the Tye River.

Today, wheelchair trails and display boards lead visitors past pictures and information about the tragedy. A trail to the left of the main display leads hikers into a two-track concrete snow shed built after the accident. The wheelchair trail continues on 2.5 miles to Windy Point. The trail ends at the Martin Creek trailhead in a total of 6 miles. (See Hike 30, Iron Goat Trail.)

The Wellington trail to the right of the display leads to the mouth of the 3-mile tunnel that was abandoned when the lower and longer tunnel to Scenic was completed. The Wellington name was changed to Tye immediately after the accident.

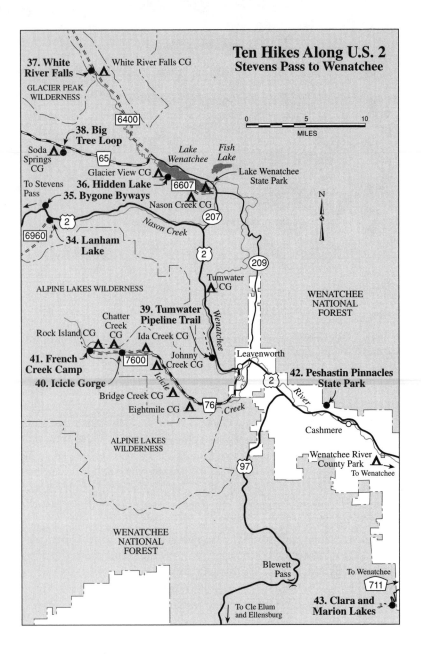

Ten Hikes Along U.S. 2
Stevens Pass to Wenatchee

37. White River Falls

White River Falls CG

GLACIER PEAK WILDERNESS

6400

38. Big Tree Loop

Soda Springs CG

65

Glacier View CG

Lake Wenatchee

Fish Lake

Lake Wenatchee State Park

36. Hidden Lake

6607

To Stevens Pass

35. Bygone Byways

Nason Creek CG

207

Nason Creek

2

6960

34. Lanham Lake

U.S. 2

209

ALPINE LAKES WILDERNESS

Tumwater CG

Wenatchee

WENATCHEE NATIONAL FOREST

N

0   5   10
MILES

39. Tumwater Pipeline Trail

Chatter Creek CG

Rock Island CG

Ida Creek CG

41. French Creek Camp

7600

Johnny Creek CG

Leavenworth

40. Icicle Gorge

Icicle

42. Peshastin Pinnacles State Park

2

River

Bridge Creek CG

Eightmile CG

76

Creek

Cashmere

ALPINE LAKES WILDERNESS

Wenatchee River County Park

To Wenatchee

WENATCHEE NATIONAL FOREST

97

Blewett Pass

To Wenatchee

711

To Cle Elum and Ellensburg

43. Clara and Marion Lakes

French Creek

TEN
HIKES ALONG
U.S. 2

STEVENS PASS TO WENATCHEE

Want to climb shards of rock, talk with an icy river, or add still more mountain lakes to your list of favorites? It's all here off U.S. 2, spur roads near Lake Wenatchee, and Forest Road 76 to Chatter Creek Ranger Station and beyond.

If you are skilled, climb the ancient spires of **Peshastin Pinnacles** (Hike 42) or just watch if you are not. If you would rather, hike down a river edge of wilderness to **White River Falls** (Hike 37) and look a waterfall in the eye. Along **Icicle Gorge** (Hike 40) explore a riverside of high rock viewpoints and places to rest and dream. Or walk through forest beside a noisy rapids to yet another trail at **French Creek Camp** (Hike 41). Or find midweek privacy in two forested lava bowls at **Clara and Marion Lakes** (Hike 43).

For information on campgrounds nearby, see Appendix 1, Campgrounds. To update reports on trail and road conditions contact the Lake Wenatchee–Leavenworth Ranger District, the Okanogan–Wenatchee National Forest. Or visit the Okanogan–Wenatchee National Forest website (see Appendix 2).

34. LANHAM LAKE

Features	▪	forest and lake
One way	▪	1.5 miles
Elevation gain	▪	1,100 feet
Difficulty	▪	moderate to steep
Open	▪	summer
Map	▪	Green Trails 144

A short trail just off U.S. 2 leads to a pleasant lake at 3,900 feet.

Drive east on U.S. 2 over Stevens Pass, turning right in about 6 miles to a snowpark area off Forest Road 6960.

(Note: To return west toward the coast on U.S. 2, turn right off Forest Road 6960 into the eastbound lane of U.S. 2, and then shortly left, downhill to the westbound lane.)

Find the signed trailhead east of Forest Road 6960 in about 50 yards, above the snowpark lot.

The path starts out in forest and in 0.5 mile breaks out into an ugly powerline right-of-way. Watch for trail signs or cairns or old tree blazes to pick your way beneath the lines to a trail again.

Lanham Lake and shoulder of Jim Hill Mountain

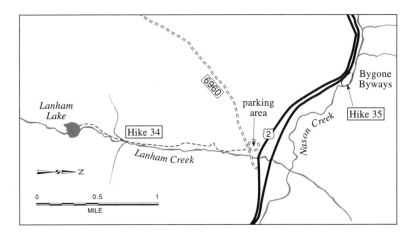

The path follows an old logging spur before entering a pleasant forest and climbing steadily near Lanham Creek to a picnic or camp spot on the lake. Can be busy on weekends.

35. BYGONE BYWAYS

Features	■	history above a raging creek
One way	■	0.25-mile loop
Elevation gain	■	about 50 feet
Difficulty	■	easy
Open	■	spring to winter
Map	■	none

Walk above noisy Nason Creek to a glimpse of the early history of rail and road transportation across Stevens Pass. Part of historic roadside displays planned in the Stevens Pass Historic District. (See also Hike 30, Iron Goat Trail; Hike 31, Deception Falls; and Hike 33, Wellington Avalanche.)

Drive east on U.S. 2 over Stevens Pass, dropping to the left from the eastbound lane to the westbound lane of U.S. 2 in about 6 miles (just beyond the snowpark area and Forest Road 6960). Find the roadside display to the right (going west) in more than a mile. (See map above.)

The path drops to a display board off the highway (get a brochure here) and then turns right down an old railroad bed blasted out of rock in 1892 by men who hand-drilled powder holes and then moved the blasted rock with horse-drawn scoops.

Bygone Byways Trail

The section of railroad here was abandoned in 1929, after the present 8-mile tunnel was built through the pass. The rail right-of-way was incorporated for a short time later as part of the first Cascade Scenic Highway.

The present-day path passes the collapsed remains of an old rock-and-earth oven used by railroad builders for baking bread, and then along a section of a tote road over the pass, built to support construction of the railway.

36. HIDDEN LAKE

Features	■	lake, forest, great scenery
One way	■	about 0.5 mile
Elevation gain	■	300 feet
Difficulty	■	short but steep
Open	■	spring to winter
Map	■	Green Trails 145

A short walk uphill past views over Lake Wenatchee leads to a pretty, boulder-bound, much photographed mountain lake.

Drive about 20 miles east of Stevens Pass on U.S. 2, turning left at Coles Corner onto Highway 207. In about 4 miles turn left toward

Hidden Lake

Wenatchee State Park and Nason Creek Campground. At the entrance to Lake Wenatchee State Park, turn sharply left onto South Shore Road, driving to the end of Forest Road 6607 at Glacier View Campground in less than 6 miles.

Find the trail off a new parking area on the left as you enter the campground. The path climbs persistently through forest with glimpses now and then down on the lake and across at Dirty Face Mountain. Huckleberries along the way in the fall, if you get there before other hikers do.

The trail ends at a point that juts out into the water, offering a full view of the lake. Unmaintained trails lead both right and left along and above the shore. Explore them all, taking care to remember where it was you started so you can find the trail back.

Tumbled rocks, some layered like huge birthday cakes, offer endless resting spots. Wonder as you rest where those rocks all tumbled from.

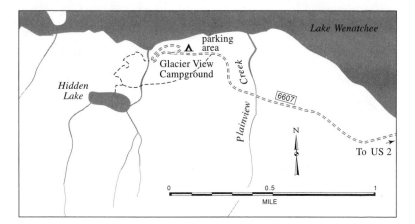

So bring a lunch, a magazine, a book, or a music tape that only you can hear and enjoy. Early mornings and late-summer evenings offer the best chance for solitude.

37. WHITE RIVER FALLS

Features ▪	waterfall, eroded rocks, forest
One way ▪	less than 1 mile
Elevation gain ▪	slight
Difficulty ▪	easy
Open ▪	summer
Map ▪	Green Trails 145

If you want to meet this waterfall full face—and it's a face worth look-ing at—take a short walk down a wilderness trail.

Drive about 20 miles east of Stevens Pass on U.S. 2, turning left at Coles Corner onto Highway 207 and following it past Lake Wenatchee State Park and down the north shore of the lake. Bear right on White River Road 6400 at its junction with the Wenatchee River Road 65. Drive 9 miles to the boundary of the Glacier Peak Wilderness Area.

Find the trail off the end of a large parking lot. The path immedi-ately crosses a bridge above a White River rapids and enters the wilder-ness. In 100 feet take a path downriver to the left on a trail signed "Panther Creek and Mount David."

An old, blazed trail makes its way above the river through big cedars and Douglas fir to an unmarked but clear junction just short of

White River Falls

a mile. The path to the left promptly snuggles up to the edge of a ledge above the river and the waterfall. Two leaping torrents drop into a pool worked only by fisherman across the river. No crossing here either above or below the falls.

As signs warn, watch small children: There are no barriers. After you've admired the falls, also admire the wondrous patterns of erosion

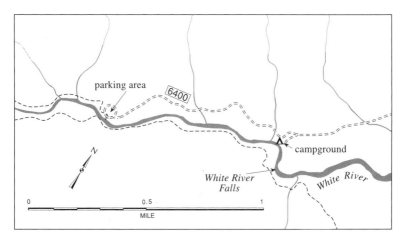

(note how even the highest boulder above the falls has been worn round by this torrent). Explore a spur path off the trail just upstream of the falls. More examples of erosion here and a view of a campground and campers across the stream. Again, do not attempt to cross the river no matter how docile the water seems.

The main wilderness trail continues down river before climbing up Panther Creek. Another steep trail goes up Mount David.

Be sure to drive into the White River Campground as you leave. Walk over the outcrops you could see from across the river. Way trails lead downstream to the fishing holes and limited views of the falls.

38. BIG TREE LOOP

Features	▪	ancient forest
One way	▪	0.5-mile loop, maybe more
Elevation gain	▪	100 feet
Difficulty	▪	easy
Open	▪	summer
Map	▪	Green Trails 145

Walk around a shady loop through old-growth forest here where you can see whatever you take the time to see. No signs. No pamphlets. Just Mother Nature dressed in her best.

Drive about 20 miles east of Stevens Pass on U.S. 2, turning left at Coles Corner onto Highway 207 and following it past Lake Wenatchee State Park down the north shore of the lake. Beyond the

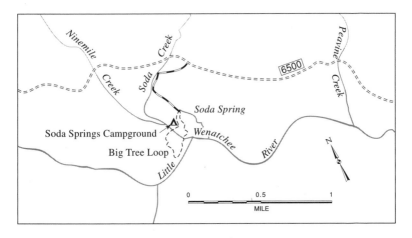

forest ranger station, bear left on Wenatchee River Road 65 at a junction with White River Road 6400. About 7 miles from the junction, turn downhill to Soda Springs Campground. Find the trail off the uphill loop at the far end of the campground road.

The path drops down to a small bridge and into a grove of old cedars, Douglas fir, and hemlock decked out with devil's club, vine maples, ferns, and flowers in season.

Not a place to hurry through. If such forests are new to you, take your plant book along so you can greet the plants you meet by name.

At the bottom of the loop, as the trail turns left, walk to the river straight ahead, return, and follow the main path through still-rich forest to another view of the river before the trail climbs gradually back to the campground.

Before you leave the campground, check the soda springs that gave the camp its name. Find the closest spring off the east side of the campground road across from the first campsite.

On an unmarked path beyond the spring and to the right, note a large, soft sandstone boulder etched with initials that's been used as a campground "register" for years. Take time to "sign in," too.

Other springs can be found on unmarked paths above and along the river.

Little Wenatchee River from Big Tree Loop

39. TUMWATER PIPELINE TRAIL

Features	■	river and history
One way	■	1 mile
Elevation gain	■	none
Difficulty	■	easy
Open	■	all year
Map	■	none

Hike an historic pipeline trail that once carried water to electric generators that powered Great Northern trains through the 8-mile Cascade Tunnel.

The pipeline and generating plant were abandoned after the railroad switched from pollution-free electricity to diesel fuel, which required the installation of giant fans in the tunnel to blow out the fumes.

Drive east on U.S. 2 into Tumwater Canyon, turning right toward the Wenatchee River on a short road leading to the river's edge, half-way between mileposts 97 and 98.

Find the trailhead off a parking lot, site of the one-time generating plant. Follow the path upriver, crossing a steel bridge that once held the water pipes. In 0.75 mile stop at a delightful sandbar with views across the river to Castle Rock, where climbers often practice on the near-vertical rock faces there.

At 1 mile, the path comes to an abrupt end at a cliff. Evidently the pipeline tunneled through rock here. A massive rockslide now blocks the opening.

Carry binoculars for watching climbers across the river. And be alert for rattlesnakes.

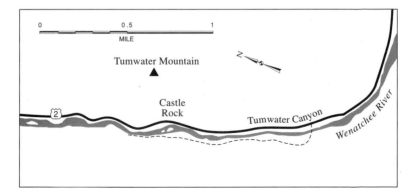

Wenatchee River and Castle Rock

40. ICICLE GORGE

Features	■	great viewpoints, forest, rushing creek
One way	■	4.5-mile loop
Elevation gain	■	very little
Difficulty	■	easy
Open	■	summer
Map	■	Green Trails 177

Hike a 4.5-mile loop on both sides of a wild and noisy mountain river, or take short hikes to viewpoints and picnic spots in a mile or less.

Drive east on U.S. 2 to Leavenworth, turning south (right) onto the Icicle Creek Road as the highway approaches the edge of town. To begin your hikes, follow the road into the Okanogan–Wenatchee National Forest (which is now Forest Road 76) and then on to the Chatter Creek Ranger Station. Or continue to a paved parking area in another 0.5 mile or to the Rock Island Campground where the road crosses Icicle Creek in another 1.5 miles.

Across from Chatter Creek Ranger Station, the loop trail drops from a parking area to a scenic bridge high above a narrow cleft of rock filled with bowls and streamlined slabs carved by Icicle Creek,

Chatter bridge over Icicle Creek

which plunges through this gorge all year long. The classic horse bridge once led pack trains to trails now in the Alpine Lakes Wilderness.

On the far side of the bridge the loop trail turns upriver (right) across several rock ledges that provide views up and down the busy creek. Beyond the bluffs the trail drops to the water's edge and wanders through rich old forest, across small creeks, and past sandy beaches with a lot of picnic and resting places. This path crosses another bridge to the Rock Island Campground before turning right and returning to the paved parking lot and the guard station.

Best parking for large vehicles is at the mid-point paved parking lot. From the parking lot, trails lead either up river to the Rock Island Campground or downstream to the Chatter Creek bridge, which offers the most interesting scenery. Warning: Wildfires in this area during 2001 may have changed the trails. Check at the ranger station.

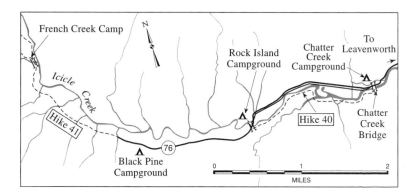

41. FRENCH CREEK CAMP

Features	▪	forest and creek
One way	▪	1.5 miles
Elevation gain	▪	very slight
Difficulty	▪	easy
Open	▪	summer
Map	▪	Green Trails 177

Take an easy walk through a shady forest up Icicle Creek to a noisy little rapids and pleasant camping spot.

Drive east on U.S. 2 to Leavenworth, turning south (right) onto Icicle Road as the highway approaches the edge of town. Follow the road into the Okanogan–Wenatchee National Forest (now Forest Road 76) and past the Chatter Creek Ranger Station. In less than 2 miles, follow the road left across the creek and then on to its end in another 2 miles. (See map on page 102.)

Icicle Creek at French Creek campground

The trail starts off the end of a parking area and proceeds straight-away toward French Creek and a well-used camping spot.

But, again, do not rush, for there's no reason here to hurry. Rather, enjoy the forest and listen—yes, listen—to the hustling creek off to your right. For before you reach the camp you'll hear a busy rapids there. Wander through the woods—you'll not get lost—and find a series of modest rapids worth seeing and listening to. Some contend you can sometimes hear voices of the past whispering to you as you wait. The spirits of hikers or explorers who came this way before? Judge from what they say to you.

The French Creek is a good destination for a test-run backpack trip. It's busy on most weekends, however. No campfires are allowed. Check with the ranger station in Leavenworth for information on 2001 wildfire damage

49. PESHASTIN PINNACLES STATE PARK

Features ■	rocky spires and mountaineers
One way ■	as far as you want to walk
Elevation gain ■	the choice is yours
Difficulty ■	easy to difficult beyond belief
Open ■	closed in winter
Map ■	trail map posted at the park

The opportunities in this state park are endless, but the limitations are enormous. You can walk on loops among this host of barren spires

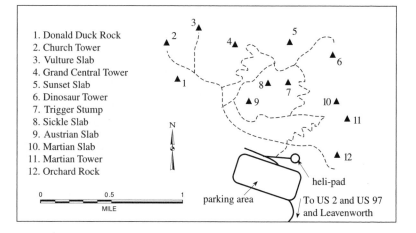

1. Donald Duck Rock
2. Church Tower
3. Vulture Slab
4. Grand Central Tower
5. Sunset Slab
6. Dinosaur Tower
7. Trigger Stump
8. Sickle Slab
9. Austrian Slab
10. Martian Slab
11. Martian Tower
12. Orchard Rock

Peshastin Pinnacles and trail

as far as you like with no problem at all. But to climb them? You'll need lessons, most certainly.

Drive east on U.S. 2 (or I-90 and U.S. 97) beyond the towns of Peshastin and Dryden (4 miles west of Cashmere) to Peshastin Pinnacles State Park on the north side of the highway. Follow signs through orchards and across an irrigation ditch to the large parking lot just below the unlikely group of barren spires—the Peshastin Pinnacles.

The trail begins at a signed display and then climbs to trails that lead to a series of loops past the base of spires with names like Dinosaur Tower (the farthest), Vulture Slab, Orchard Rock, Grand Central Tower, Martian Slab, and Austrian Slab, to name a few.

This park, nothing more than rock spires of cracks and slabs, has been used for years by rock climbers to learn, practice, and test their skills belaying, rappelling, climbing slabs, jamming holds, and working cracks with their static and dynamic ropes and assorted tools like carabiners, cams, nuts, tubers, hammers, brakes, harnesses, and shoes.

Not that you have to climb here to enjoy this park. Just watching and listening can be interesting, too, as climbers talk to each other across this face or up that crack in places that seem impossible to reach.

So walk, look, and listen, remembering not to interfere with those climbing or with their ropes that sometimes dangle loosely on the trail. And stand clear of all the rock spires in case some piece of climbing hardware happens to be dropped.

43. CLARA AND MARION LAKES

Features ■	mountain lakes in lava scree
One way ■	a long mile
Elevation gain ■	about 900 feet
Difficulty ■	steep
Open ■	summer
Map ■	Okanogan–Wenatchee National Forest map

Here is a twin surprise: two small mountain lakes surrounded by ponderosa pine set in bowls of lava scree typical of area mountains.

Drive east to Wenatchee on either U.S. 2 or I-90 and U.S. 97, following signs straight through town to the Mission Ridge Ski Resort, 12 miles past the edge of town. Great views of the Columbia River valley and Wenatchee from the road.

Find the trail, marked as the "Squilchuck Trail/Lake Clara," uphill to the right where the paved road first enters the ski area parking lot.

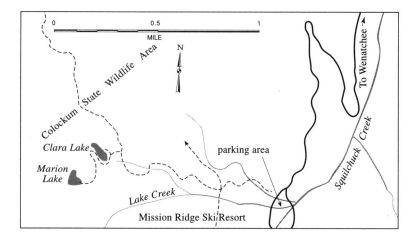

Trail bikes are permitted on the first section of the trail, as ruts in the path and trenches on steep switchbacks attest.

At a T junction, signed with definitions of trail uses but with no directions, turn left on a broad path that serves snowmobiles in the winter and then in a few yards turns sharply uphill to the right.

The path now climbs through pleasant forest (no motor bikers allowed now) to a second T junction. Turn left here, cross a creek, pass a shallow, narrow pond, and shortly reach the outlet of Clara Lake.

Inviting places to camp and picnic in the trees or in the sun on both sides of the lake, at 5,500 feet.

To reach Marion Lake, cross the outlet at Clara Lake, walk up the lake to a clump of trees, and take a 0.25-mile trail that traverses back uphill over a ridge and down to Marion Lake, also at 5,500 feet, set in a bowl of its own.

Linger near either or both. Such open pleasantness is hard to find.

Clara Lake

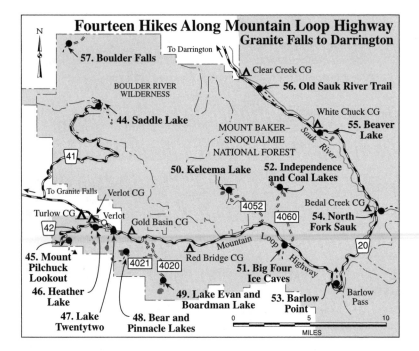

Fourteen Hikes Along Mountain Loop Highway
Granite Falls to Darrington

N

57. Boulder Falls

To Darrington

BOULDER RIVER WILDERNESS

44. Saddle Lake

Clear Creek CG

56. Old Sauk River Trail

White Chuck CG

55. Beaver Lake

MOUNT BAKER–SNOQUALMIE NATIONAL FOREST

41

To Granite Falls

Verlot CG

50. Kelcema Lake

52. Independence and Coal Lakes

Sauk River

Bedal Creek CG

Turlow CG

Verlot

42

45. Mount Pilchuck Lookout

46. Heather Lake

Gold Basin CG

4052

4060

54. North Fork Sauk

20

Mountain Loop Highway

Red Bridge CG

51. Big Four Ice Caves

Barlow Pass

4021

4020

49. Lake Evan and Boardman Lake

53. Barlow Point

47. Lake Twentytwo

48. Bear and Pinnacle Lakes

0   5   10

MILES

Big Four Ice Caves

FOURTEEN HIKES ALONG MOUNTAIN LOOP HIGHWAY

GRANITE FALLS TO DARRINGTON

Too much to list here: eleven mountain lakes, each worth every minute of your time to camp near or hike around in forest, in high meadows, some with beavers, too. Plus the **Mount Pilchuck Lookout** (Hike 45) with views of all of the high surrounding peaks. **Big Four Ice Caves** (Hike 51) must be seen. Take a leisurely walk down the original **Old Sauk River Trail** (Hike 56) that has survived with all its trees and flowers intact despite the threatening river. And follow a lush rainforest-like trail that leads past a salty pond on the **North Fork Sauk** (Hike 54). Visit the North Fork waterfall en route.

For information on campgrounds nearby, see Appendix 1, Campgrounds. For the latest reports on trail and road conditions telephone the Darrington Ranger District, the Verlot Public Service Center, or use the Mount Baker–Snoqualmie National Forest website (see Appendix 2).

44. SADDLE LAKE

Features	■	lake and meadows
One way	■	2-plus miles
Elevation gain	■	700 feet
Difficulty	■	steep and rough
Open	■	summer
Maps	■	Green Trails 109, 110

Struggle 2 miles to a subalpine lake that marks the entrance to an inspiring world of alpine meadows.

From I-5 in Everett, turn east at Exit 194 onto U.S. 2 (from I-405 turn off at Exit 23 to Highway 522), turning north in both instances onto Highway 9. About 6 miles north of U.S. 2, turn east on Highway 92 to Granite Falls and the beginning of Mountain Loop Highway in another 8 miles.

In about 7 miles from Granite Falls (or 4 miles west of the Verlot Public Service Center), turn north onto Forest Road 41, following the road some 17 miles to Tupso Pass. Find the trail at the end of Spur Road 4160.

The trail enters the Boulder River Wilderness and promptly begins its rooted and eroded struggle up switchbacks to a ridge (scenery now and then) and Saddle Lake at 3,780 feet.

Admire the lake with its marsh-loving flowers and scurrying salamanders and then press on at least another mile (this path is not so rough) to the first of many rolling meadows tucked with tarns.

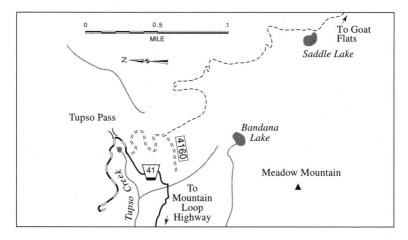

Storm-bent tree near Saddle Lake

Find your own hummock of heather and give thanks to the hundreds who did political battle to preserve this corner of heaven.

To add further thanks for an even bigger corner of this paradise, hike another 1.5 miles to Goat Flats—a decorated altar of nature's splendors. And, yes, treat all of these tarns and meadows with the respect due every place of worship. No open fires.

45. MOUNT PILCHUCK LOOKOUT

Features	▪	panorama after panorama from 5,300 feet
One way	▪	3 miles
Elevation gain	▪	2,200 feet
Difficulty	▪	a very steep, short boulder field
Open	▪	snow often until late summer
Map	▪	Green Trails 109

Panoramas here (maybe the best in this book) from the Olympics to the Cascades plus everything in between. But not for the timid or the unprepared.

Mount Pilchuck Lookout

To reach Mountain Loop Highway, drive north on Highway 9 for 6 miles from U.S. 2, or south 12 miles from Arlington, to Highway 92 and then east to Granite Falls in 8 more miles.

From Granite Falls, follow Mountain Loop Highway a little more than 12 miles to the Verlot Public Service Center. Turn right (south) onto Forest Road 42 in another mile (just beyond the bridge over the south fork of the Stillaguamish River), driving about 7 miles to a large parking area. Find the trail uphill to the right at the beginning of the parking lot.

The path climbs most of the way in forest with glimpses of surrounding country through the trees and then loses elevation as it works its way around cliffs.

Don't be lured by well-worn jogs in the trail that may seem time-saving shortcuts through boulder fields. No way. First, the rock fields can be dangerous. And second, you may very well lose your way, particularly coming down with few cairns to guide you. These unmarked slopes are pocked with cliffs.

The trail ends in a final series of switchbacks that climb 100 feet to a final pile of giant boulders topped with the lookout. Pick your way to the building with care.

Again, stick with the trail, avoid the lure of shortcuts across the boulder fields, and use the time you might think you would save to enjoy what you see. Take a highway map to identify what you're looking at (a forest map will help but is much too small).

The trail starts in the national forest and ends in state park land.

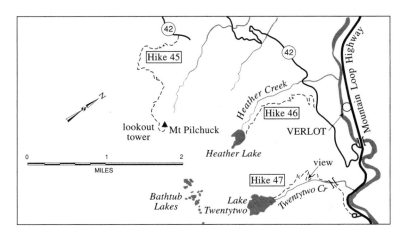

46. HEATHER LAKE

Features	▪	pretty mountain lake
One way	▪	2 miles
Elevation gain	▪	1,000 feet
Difficulty	▪	moderate to steep
Open	▪	summer
Map	▪	Green Trails 109

Hike through old forest, past a small waterfall, to an alpine lake tucked in a cirque on the side of Mount Pilchuck.

On Highway 9, drive north 6 miles from U.S. 2 or south 12 miles from Arlington to Highway 92 and then east to Granite Falls in 8 more miles.

From Granite Falls, follow Mountain Loop Highway a little more than 12 miles to the Verlot Public Service Center. Turn right (south) in another mile onto Forest Road 42 (just beyond the bridge over the south fork of the Stillaguamish River). Find the trail to the left in less than 1.5 miles, uphill across from a parking area on the right side of the road. (See map above.)

The path (no longer up an old logging road) starts with a series of short switchbacks up a stream draw through maturing second-growth

Heather Lake

forest. Note the huge old stumps of trees, 6 to 10 feet in diameter, logged here early in the twentieth century by men who stood on spring-boards jammed into the notches you can still see in the stumps.

The trail joins a stretch of the old road but shortly resumes its trail-like ways, climbing to a small waterfall (catch your breath here) and then switchbacking again before dropping to the lake at 2,450 feet.

Limited camping is permitted here away from the lakeshore. Fisherman trails lead around the lake. A lot of rocks to sit on to watch and listen to what Nature has hidden here.

47. LAKE TWENTYTWO

Features	■ waterfalls and lake
One way	■ 2.5 miles or less
Elevation gain	■ 1,200 feet or less
Difficulty	■ steep
Open	■ summer
Maps	■ Green Trails 109, 110

A hike to the lake is certainly worth the effort, but a walk halfway through a lovely forest past waterfalls is a worthy effort, too.

On Highway 9, drive north 6 miles from U.S. 2, or south 12 miles from Arlington, to Highway 92 and then east to Granite Falls in 8 more miles.

From Granite Falls, follow Mountain Loop Highway a little more than 12 miles to the Verlot Public Service Center. Find the trailhead in less than 2 miles at the end of a short spur road loop to the right. (See map on page 113.)

The path almost immediately enters a research natural area that, except for the damage created by humans along the trail, has evolved untouched as a lush old-growth forest filled with fallen moss-covered giants, old trees straddling rocks, and seedlings bursting from rotting logs, amid an abundance of salmonberries, maidenhair, deer and lady ferns, devil's club, bunchberry, skunk cabbages, and even shy single delights on mossy logs—just to begin a list.

Note, too, as you walk the beginning section of trail how even in the driest years little streams bubble from rocks above the path, demonstrating how an established and undisturbed forest stabilizes water runoff, which dries up early in the summer on exposed logged-off trails.

The trail winds above the highway for an easy 0.5 mile to a bridge over Twentytwo Creek. Pause here for sure to enjoy the beauty of the busy little waterfalls and to follow short way paths through the pools and giant cedar trees.

Lake 22 Trail

Beyond the creek, the trail starts its stiff upward climb toward the lake in another 2 miles. Half that distance, however, will reward you with still more opportunities to admire trees, shrubs, and flowers before coming face to face with a pretty, full-scale, two-step waterfall. For many, that may be destination enough.

For those who climb on, though, a pretty lake lies at 2,460 feet with an almost permanent snowfield at the end. On weekends, of course, hundreds of people, too. No open fires are permitted here. And, please, treat the fragile lakeshore most tenderly.

48. BEAR AND PINNACLE LAKES

Features	■	lakes and forest
One way	■	2 miles or less
Elevation gain	■	up to 1,200 feet
Difficulty	■	moderate to steep
Open	■	midsummer
Maps	■	Green Trails 109, 110

An easy 0.25-mile walk leads to one mountain lake set in forest. An added 2-mile uphill struggle leads to another set in a heather cirque. Both are worth the trip.

On Highway 9, drive north 6 miles from U.S. 2, or south 12 miles from Arlington, to Highway 92 and then east to Granite Falls in 8 more miles.

From Granite Falls, drive east on Mountain Loop Highway past the Verlot Information Station and Gold Basin Campground. About 2.5 miles beyond the campground, turn right (south) on Forest Road 4020, turning right in another 2.3 miles onto Forest Road 4021. Follow Forest Road 4021 another 3.4 miles to the trailhead on the left.

The trail starts with a short, steep pitch that ends in about 50 feet at the base of a huge cedar snag and then continues on to a junction. Turn right at the trail junction in a few hundred yards to reach Bear Lake (2,775 feet), and left to Pinnacle Lake in another 2 miles.

The trail to Bear Lake follows a ridge with views over the logged-off Stillaguamish Valley before dropping through open forest past several camp spots on two levels above the lake.

No sandy beaches here, but a muddy wade will lead to a midday swim in warm water over icy springs. Watch for ospreys fishing here. Fishing paths lead around the lake.

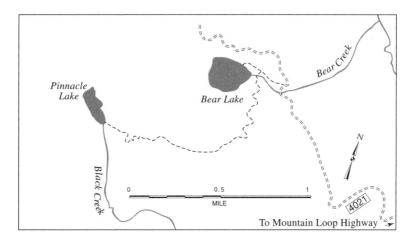

The trail to Pinnacle Lake, which can be soggy in the spring, climbs to views over Bear Lake, topping out across a series of marshy flower and huckleberry meadows before reaching the lake (3,800 feet) surrounded by patches of timber, more meadows, and scenic rock bluffs. Treat the meadows here with kindness so others after you may enjoy them too.

Pinnacle Lake

49. LAKE EVAN AND BOARDMAN LAKE

Features	▪	rich forest and lovely lakes
One way	▪	1 mile
Elevation gain	▪	200 feet
Difficulty	▪	easy to moderate
Open	▪	summer
Map	▪	Green Trails 110

Two mountain lakes in less than a mile, plus grand old-growth forest worth the trip all by itself.

On Highway 9 drive north 6 miles from U.S. 2, or south 12 miles from Arlington, to Highway 92 and then east to Granite Falls in 8 more miles.

From Granite Falls, continue east on Mountain Loop Highway past the Verlot Information Station and Gold Basin Campground. About 2.5 miles beyond the campground, turn south on Forest Road 4020, reaching the trailhead (views over the valley en route) in about 4.7 miles. Find a parking area as the road jogs sharply to the west.

Find the heavily used trail beyond the down roadside of Evan Creek. The path reaches Lake Evan (2,751 feet) with its soggy but heavily used camping spots in less than 50 yards beyond a grove of old cedar trees.

To reach Boardman Lake (2,981 feet) take the trail uphill through a lush, open forest of old-growth Douglas fir, hemlock, and cedars that have grown here for hundreds of years. Wonder as you stand in awe below them: Should they be cut, could the two or three seedlings

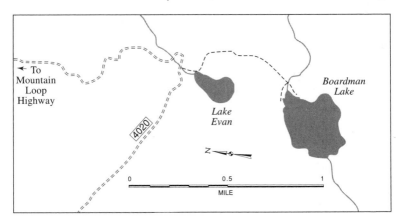

Boardman Lake

loggers promise to plant in each one's place ever truly replace them? In the 50 years they brag about? Never. In 200 years—at the end of six generations, for your great-great-great-great grandchildren? At this elevation? Probably not even then.

The trail crests a ridge above the outlet creek and then drops to the lake. Go either right or left for picnic or camping spots. The trail to the left crosses the outlet and then circles a rocky knoll.

No warning seems necessary here. The trail is wide and easy to follow. Yet each year novice hikers lose their way trying the return to the road. So note where the trail reaches the lake and if you decide to return to the car alone have a friend verify your starting path on the well-worn trail.

50. KELCEMA LAKE

Features ■	mountain lake
One way ■	less than 0.5 mile
Elevation gain ■	slight
Difficulty ■	easy
Open ■	midsummer
Map ■	Green Trails 110

A narrow and steep road leads to an easy trail that continues on to a popular lake just inside the Boulder River Wilderness.

On Highway 9, drive north 6 miles from U.S. 2, or south 12 miles from Arlington, to Highway 92 and then east to Granite Falls in 8 more miles.

From Granite Falls, drive east on Mountain Loop Highway, turning north on Forest Road 4052 about 1 mile beyond (east of) Silverton. (The road is sometimes not signed at the highway nor along the road itself.) Find the trail in about 4.5 miles up a view road that can be rough beyond a "paved" crossing of Deer Creek, which may run high in the spring.

Kelcema Lake

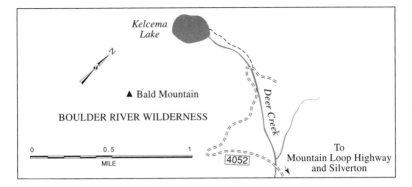

The trail begins on the left side of the road at a point where the road turns sharply right. The path winds through a soggy meadow and open forest to the lake at 3,182 feet in a cirque at the base of Bald Mountain to the south.

Long before the road was built, this area was used as a Boy Scout camp. Nature now slowly heals itself. But don't let past human abuses now excuse your own. Campsites in well-worn places among the rocks.

51. BIG FOUR ICE CAVES

Features	■	ice cave
One way	■	1 mile
Elevation gain	■	200 feet
Difficulty	■	moderate
Open	■	summer
Map	■	Green Trails 110

Ice caves! What else is there to say? Caves (some years just one) etched by streams beneath the snow and ice of a not-quite glacier at the shaded base of Big Four Mountain that commands this section of Mountain Loop Highway.

From Granite Falls, drive 15 miles east beyond the Verlot Public Service Center on the Mountain Loop Highway. Two marked spur roads, 0.25 mile apart, lead right off the highway to two different trailheads.

See the best spectacle from the first parking area. A hotel, built in 1922 for tourists brought in by train, once occupied this site. The hotel burned in 1949; a chimney is all that now remains. As you stand in the hotel clearing, you can see why they built the resort here and

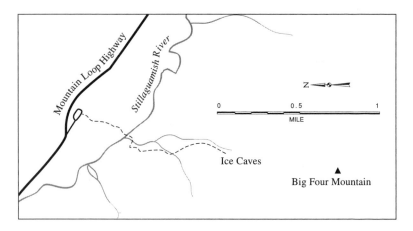

wonder, truly, why it failed. For now as then, waterfalls plume in strings from Big Four's cliffs. Now as then, birds sing in the underbrush and trees. Now as then, beaver try to dam the ponds, and now as then, they are just as difficult to see.

The second parking area does not offer a vista. Trails from each site, however, join in 0.25 mile and continue to the ice caves.

Big Four Ice Cave

Planked walkways now lead across soggy meadows at the trails' start, and a sturdy bridge now spans a creek to a view of the caves at the trail's end.

With the same warnings now, most certainly, as hotel guests got: The caves are hazardous, as is the snowfield atop them. The snow and ice here fall from mountain cliffs in the winter. Rocks fall from the cliffs in the summer. Explore with caution. Don't walk atop or inside the caves. Check with the Verlot Information Station for current conditions and obey any and all warning signs.

52. INDEPENDENCE AND COAL LAKES

Features	▪	lakes and old forest
One way	▪	0.75 mile but seems much farther
Elevation gain	▪	200 feet (counting the ups and downs)
Difficulty	▪	steep and rough
Open	▪	summer
Map	▪	Green Trails 110

Independence Lake is the goal here—with Coal Lake an extra prize. Plus—yes, plus—spectacular aerial views of Big Four Mountain and the Stillaguamish Valley from the ever-climbing road.

From Granite Falls, 8 miles east of Highway 9, drive east on Mountain Loop Highway about 15.5 miles beyond the Verlot Public Service Center, turning left (north) to Forest Road 4060 (the first road beyond the road to the well-signed ice caves, see Hike 51). The junction

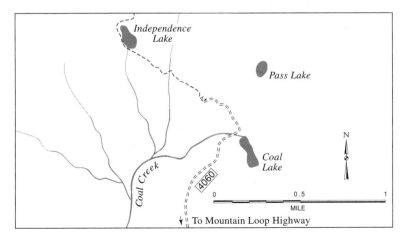

Independence Lake

may not be signed, and there may be no forest road numbers posted on the road. Stop at a formal viewpoint in about 3 miles. (See the sights and then look for black leaf-imprinted rocks in ancient shale across the road.)

The road passes a Coal Lake parking strip on the left at about 4.5 miles, reaching the end of the road and the Independence Lake trailhead parking area in another twisty, uphill 0.25 mile.

Find the trail to Independence Lake uphill from the road-end parking lot. Again, there may be no signs. The path starts out in an old clear-cut but shortly enters a cool and shady old-growth forest.

Once it enters the old forest, the trail reverts to history. Probably built by the Civilian Conservation Corps in the 1930s, the path is largely unchanged. Follow still-visible, overgrown blazes on trees as the trail drops down to a creek, makes its way back up again, goes level for a while to another creek, and then climbs sharply in lunging spurts over roots and rocks to the jewel of a lake at 3,700 feet.

Resting slabs beside the outlet creek make the whole trip worthwhile. Listen here for the grouse, chatter of the squirrels and chipmunks, and one-note trill of the varied thrush.

The trail continues on around the crystal blue lake to an open meadow with camp spots in the trees.

And yes, as you drive back, take time to walk the few short yards from the road over a ledge to the narrow, snow-fed Coal Lake, surrounded by steep rock and timber slopes, at 3,420 feet. If you brought your kayak, canoe, or rubber raft: Enjoy!

53. BARLOW POINT

Features	■	vistas
One way	■	1.25 miles
Elevation gain	■	800 feet
Difficulty	■	moderate to very steep
Open	■	summer
Map	■	Green Trails 111

Walk an easy 0.25 mile and then climb a steep switchback mile to views out over the Stillaguamish Valley, down on Monte Cristo Lakes, and out at Big Four, Dickerman, and Sheep Mountains.

From Granite Falls, drive east on Mountain Loop Highway about 19.4 miles beyond the Verlot Public Service Center to Barlow Pass. Park either on the highway or in a small parking area at the end of a short spur road to the left. Find the trail off the parking area.

The path starts out on a gradual traverse through forest before turning right to begin the grinding switchback climb to the rocky site of an abandoned lookout at 3,300 feet.

The first section of the walk follows part of the bed of the railroad that once led to the long-defunct, but still private, Monte Cristo mining complex at the end of the now-gated county road (to the right) at the pass. The trail once continued down the railroad grade above the highway toward Silverton for almost 2 miles. No water, naturally.

Barlow Point

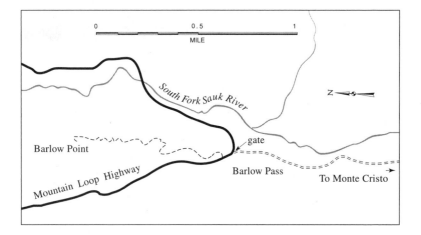

54. NORTH FORK SAUK

Features	▪	a waterfall and old-growth forest
One way	▪	2 miles or less
Elevation gain	▪	200 feet
Difficulty	▪	moderate
Open	▪	early spring
Map	▪	Green Trails 111

There are two close and easy features here. The first is the North Fork waterfall as you start your drive up the north fork of the Sauk River. The second is the easy wander through the lush forest near the primitive Sloan Creek Campground.

From Seattle drive north on I-5, turn east at Exit 208, and follow Highway 530 through Arlington to Darrington. Turn south in Darrington to Mountain Loop Highway, driving about 18 miles (or about 7 miles north of Barlow Pass if you start the loop from Granite Falls) to North Fork Road 49, sharply uphill to the east, just north of the North Fork Guard Station.

In a mile, park and hike down a steep, short trail (less than 0.25 mile) to see North Fork Falls. Find the trail off a small parking area on the right side of the road. A torrent all year and a tumult in the spring. Take your camera. The trail ends at a viewpoint. Stay on the trail.

Drive another 6 miles from the falls to a spur road on the left into the primitive Sloan Creek Campground. (If you cross the bridge over the river you've gone too far.)

North Fork Falls

Step out of your car and immerse yourself in a lush pocket of grand and ancient old-growth Douglas fir and cedar trees and old snags pecked full of holes, all rising out of a lush understory of ferns, devil's club, twisted stalk, foam flowers—and that's just the beginning.

Walk 100 yards or so down the North Fork trail to find a rusty salt-lick mineral seep off to the left in a skunk cabbage garden where animals come to drink the witches' brew. Animal tracks—and deer if you're lucky—all of the time.

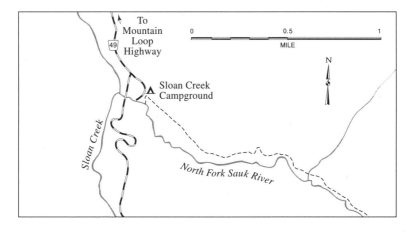

The trail continues up the North Fork, entering the Glacier Peak Wilderness in about 0.5 mile. Once in the wilderness the path climbs away from the river across old avalanche tracks with views occasionally up to Sloan Peak. Walk as far as you want.

55. BEAVER LAKE

Features	▪	beaver ponds
One way	▪	3 miles but you need not go that far
Elevation gain	▪	very little
Difficulty	▪	easy
Open	▪	all year
Map	▪	Green Trails 111

An easy 2-mile walk over an old abandoned logging railroad grade leads to a small beaver lake and a haven for birds and other wildlife.

From Seattle drive north on I-5, turn east at Exit 208, and follow Highway 530 through Arlington to Darrington. Turn south in Darrington to Mountain Loop Highway.

At 10 miles, cross the Sauk River and find the trail off a short spur road to the right just beyond the river bridge and across from the junction with Forest Road 23 and its bridge over the White Chuck River and the abandoned White Chuck Campground.

Beaver here with wood ducks, goldeneyes, deer, and mallards—if you are quiet and careful.

The path starts south out of the parking area on an old railroad

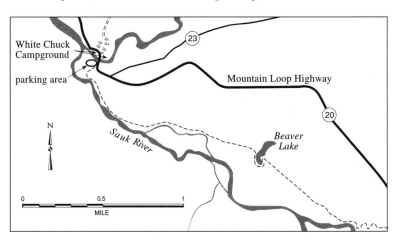

Sauk River on Beaver Lake Trail

grade built in 1914 (you'll find signs of an old trestle later on), passing occasional big hemlocks and cedar trees with feasts of salmonberries amongst the nettles in early summer.

Shortly, the trail drops to the left of the railroad grade to follow a sometimes soggy off-and-on puncheon path to a small bridge and pond and your first glimpses of the beavers' work. Old overgrown dams survive amid signs of current beaver upkeep and repair on weakening sections of the pond. With verdant groves of old cedars to the right.

Wander paths atop the old beaver dams as far as they allow. Spring floods change the landscape here almost every year. The trail ends at the road but a walk back the way you came is more interesting.

56. OLD SAUK RIVER TRAIL

Features ■ grand old-growth forest plus a river
One way ■ 3 miles
Elevation gain ■ none
Difficulty ■ easy
Open ■ all year
Map ■ Green Trails 110

Walk slowly here. Listen to the old Sauk River. Admire its power. See its history etched in the eroded shore. Note the ancient trees and flowers that now thrive abundantly as they await another flood. All this from a 3-mile trail that is almost flat.

From Seattle drive north on I-5, turn east at Exit 208, and follow Highway 530 through Arlington to Darrington. Turn south in Darrington to Mountain Loop Highway. Find a hiker trail sign and parking area in the trees to the left about 0.7 mile beyond the bridge over Clear Creek and Clear Creek Campground. If you drive the loop highway from Granite Falls, watch for the trailhead on the right about 5 miles from the bridge over the Sauk River just beyond White Chuck Campground.

The trail wends its way through continuing groves of old cedar and hemlock filled with arches of moss-draped vine maple. The old floodplain, just a few feet above the river, bursts with forest flowers in season: in the spring, star flowers, trilliums, and lilies, with bunchberries, red-tasseled devil's club, and blossoming pipsissewas in the fall. With sword ferns, deer ferns, and licorice ferns, of course.

The Sauk River, as the age of the trees here testify, created this floodplain hundreds of years ago and is still cutting the bank away as

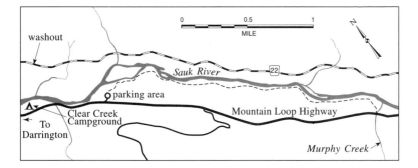

it swings back and forth across the wide riverbed. Note the exposed polished monster boulders still being shaped in the ever-changing channels and wonder from whence they came and how they ever got that far.

And yes, watch the shouting kayakers drift past from their upriver landing near the old White Chuck Campground.

Sauk River

57. BOULDER FALLS

Features	■	waterfalls and old-growth forest
One way	■	1.25 miles
Elevation gain	■	200 feet
Difficulty	■	easy with one short grade
Open	■	early spring to late fall
Maps	■	Green Trails 77, 109

Walk through lush forest to double wisps of water pluming off a cliff into the raging Boulder River in the Boulder River Wilderness.

From Seattle drive north on I-5, turn east at Exit 208, and follow Highway 530 through Arlington to milepost 41, about 8 miles west of Darrington.

At the milepost sign, turn south onto what is sometimes signed as French Creek Road 2010, driving past an abandoned campground to the end of the road in 4 miles.

Find the trail off the end of the parking area. Trail sign in about 100 yards.

The path starts on an overgrown logging road through a verdant alder forest with only glimpses of the river through the trees. The trail remains level until it turns uphill, climbing past a camp spot and the skeleton of an old shelter well above the river to the right.

At the wilderness boundary, the path enters old-growth forest but stays well above the river. Listen for the real Boulder Falls out of sight below you in the gully. (No trail.)

You'll hear the popular unnamed double falls (often thought of as Boulder Falls) plunging from its cliff well before you reach a resting

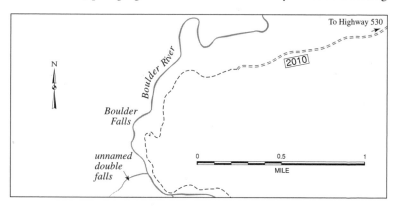

Boulder River and unnamed falls

log with a full view of the falls directly across the river. Walk to an open area in another 50 yards to find way paths down to the river and new perspectives of the falls, which flow all summer even in the driest years. Another path drops to the river just before you reach the resting log, but offers no views of the falls.

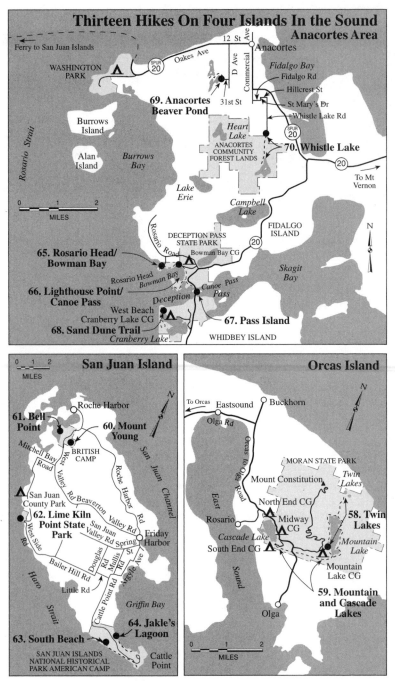

Thirteen Hikes On Four Islands In the Sound
Anacortes Area

Ferry to San Juan Islands

12 St

Oakes Ave

Anacortes

WASHINGTON PARK

SPUR 20

D Ave

Commercial

Fidalgo Bay

Fidalgo Rd

Hillcrest St

St Mary's Dr

Whistle Lake Rd

31st St

69. Anacortes Beaver Pond

Burrows Island

Burrows Bay

Rosario Strait

Alan Island

Heart Lake

ANACORTES COMMUNITY FOREST LANDS

SPUR 20

70. Whistle Lake

(20)

To Mt Vernon

Lake Erie

Campbell Lake

FIDALGO ISLAND

N

0   1   2
MILES

Rosario Road

DECEPTION PASS STATE PARK

Bowman Bay CG

Skagit Bay

65. Rosario Head/ Bowman Bay

Rosario Head

Bowman Bay

20

66. Lighthouse Point/ Canoe Pass

Canoe Pass

Pass

Deception Pass

West Beach

Cranberry Lake CG

67. Pass Island

68. Sand Dune Trail

Cranberry Lake

WHIDBEY ISLAND

San Juan Island

0   1   2
MILES

N

Roche Harbor

61. Bell Point

60. Mount Young

Mitchell Bay Road

West Valley Rd

BRITISH CAMP

San Juan Channel

Roche Harbor Rd

San Juan County Park

62. Lime Kiln Point State Park

West Side Rd

Beaverton Valley Rd

San Juan Valley Rd

Spring St

Friday Harbor

Bailer Hill Rd

Douglas Rd

Mullis Rd

Argyle Ave

Little Rd

Cattle Point Rd

Griffin Bay

Haro Strait

63. South Beach

64. Jakle's Lagoon

SAN JUAN ISLANDS NATIONAL HISTORICAL PARK AMERICAN CAMP

Cattle Point

Orcas Island

N

To Orcas

Eastsound

Buckhorn

Olga Rd

Orcas to Olga Road

MORAN STATE PARK

Twin Lakes

Mount Constitution

58. Twin Lakes

North End CG

Rosario

East Sound

Midway CG

Cascade Lake

South End CG

Mountain Lake

Mountain Lake CG

59. Mountain and Cascade Lakes

Olga

0   1   2
MILES

Deception Pass Bridge

THIRTEEN HIKES ON FOUR ISLANDS IN THE SOUND

ORCAS, SAN JUAN, FIDALGO, AND WHIDBEY ISLANDS

Orcas Island offers mountains. San Juan Island, whales, high views, and forts. Fidalgo Island, lakes. And in Deception Pass State Park, between Whidbey and Fidalgo Islands, there are still more islands in every shape and form.

On Orcas Island enjoy trails along creeks and around lakes in totally inland **Moran State Park** (Hikes 58 and 59). On San Juan Island hike to grand vistas from **Mount Young** (Hike 60) and then watch orca whales from rocks around **Lime Kiln Lighthouse** (Hike 62). On Fidalgo Island visit the City of **Anacortes Beaver Pond** (Hike 69) on the very edge of town. And at Deception Pass State Park on Whidbey Island start your tour with a scenic stroll from **Rosario Head to Bowman Bay** (Hike 65) before picking from a list of other paths, every one worthwhile.

For information on campgrounds nearby, see Appendix 1, Campgrounds. For the latest reports on trail and road conditions telephone the Washington State Parks Information Center (see Appendix 2).

58. TWIN LAKES

Orcas Island

Features	▪	lakes and forest
One way	▪	2.25 miles
Elevation gain	▪	200 feet
Difficulty	▪	moderate
Open	▪	all year
Map	▪	Moran State Park brochure

A gentle trail winds along the shore of one lake before climbing gradually up a cool, shallow valley to two pleasant, smaller mountain lakes.

Take the state ferry at the west end of North Cascades Highway 20 in Anacortes to Orcas Island. From the Orcas Island ferry landing, follow signs for 13 miles through Eastsound to Moran State Park. Note: During the summer, those camping are required to have advance reservations. See Appendix 1, Campgrounds.

Twin Lake and Mount Constitution

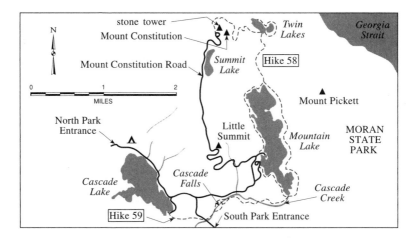

From the park entrance, continue along the shore of Cascade Lake toward Olga, turning uphill to the left in 1.5 miles onto the road to Mount Constitution (be sure to visit the vista tower there) and then right on a spur road to Mountain Lake in another mile. Find the trail to the left of the boat ramp in Mountain Lake Campground.

The path ambles along the west shore of the lake around coves and points mostly near the water, through groves of old trees and past unmarked paths to viewpoints and picnic spots.

At one point the trail skirts a blown down area, which illustrates the violence of the winter storms that sometimes sweep the island. At another point it passes a meadow, site of someone's home in the past.

At the upper end of the lake, in a little more than 1.25 miles, the trail drops down to a bridge and trail junction: left to Twin Lakes, right around Mountain Lake.

The broad Twin Lakes path now makes its way gradually upward through rich forest, past a rocky cliff, always within earshot of a busy creek, to another junction in about 0.75 mile in a grand stand of ancient Douglas fir and young hemlock surrounded by ferns and flowers with pileated woodpeckers and grazing deer.

Turn right there to both lakes and the small stream that connects them. Enjoy the forest and view of the lakes or take trails across a wooden bridge—left around the little lake in about 0.5 mile or right around the larger in more than 0.5 mile. The path that continues ahead climbs sharply about 1.25 miles through second-growth forest to the tower atop Mount Constitution. Views from the tower there never end.

59. MOUNTAIN AND CASCADE LAKES

Orcas Island

Features ■	waterfalls and forest
One way ■	3-plus miles
Elevation loss ■	570 feet
Difficulty ■	moderate
Open ■	all year
Map ■	Moran State Park brochure

Waterfalls and rich old forest: all along a single trail that drops from Mountain Lake to Cascade Lake. Have someone drop you off at the top and pick you up at the bottom.

Take the state ferry at the west end of North Cascades Highway 20 in Anacortes. From the Orcas Island ferry landing, follow signs for 13 miles through Eastsound to Moran State Park. Note: During the summer, those camping are required to have advance reservations. See Appendix 1, Campgrounds.

From the park entrance continue along the shore of Cascade Lake toward Olga, turning uphill to the left in 1.5 miles onto the road to Mount Constitution and then right on a spur road to Mountain Lake in another mile. (See map on page 137.)

Find the signed trail off the right side of the road as you first reach the Mountain Lake landing complex.

The path winds through forest, dropping below the lake's outlet dam in less than a mile. At the dam, the trail drops downhill on the left side of the outlet stream (deer here in all the unexpected places), crossing back to the right in another 0.25 mile. At the end of 1.5 miles, the path crosses a bridge at the end of an alder-rimmed meadow and breaks out onto a road. In another long 0.25 mile, turn left downhill off the road onto a trail signed to Cavern, Rustic, and Cascade Falls.

The trail now switchbacks down to above the first falls (way trails lead to closer looks) and passes through a grove of impressive cedars and Douglas firs soaking their roots near the creek, reaching the second falls at the end of 1.75 miles.

At Cascade Falls, the largest, in another few hundred yards, the trail drops past a series of three cascades, all with informal viewing points.

A warning here: Moss-covered rocks can be dangerous and slippery when wet. Not a place for children.

Cascade Falls

To continue to Cascade Lake, take the lower, well-developed trail along the wooden rail (uphill paths lead to a parking area on the road). The trail drops through still more groves of ancient trees before reaching the highway.

At the highway turn right and in about 100 yards, look back over your shoulder to see an osprey nest on a broken tree top. Cross to a parking area and a gated road that leads to the Cascade Lake ranger station and camp.

60. MOUNT YOUNG

San Juan Island

Features	■	sweeping views and historic site
One way	■	1 mile
Elevation gain	■	about 600 feet
Difficulty	■	short but steep
Open	■	all year
Map	■	San Juan Island National Historical Park brochure

Views over farms, bays, and inlets at Haro Strait and out over the Olympics from atop a glacier-rounded "mountain." With a quiet reminder of the violence of the beautiful surrounding sea in a small military cemetery en route.

Take the state ferry to San Juan Island at the end of North Cascades Highway 20 in Anacortes. From the San Juan Island ferry terminal in Friday Harbor, follow signs toward Roche Harbor. Turn south toward British Camp at a T junction in about 9 miles to the northern half of the San Juan Island National Historical Park.

After visiting the garden and restored buildings of the British fort (the British here stood off a 66-man American army during a 12-year dispute over who had jurisdiction over the shooting of a pig), find the mountain trail through the trees off the end of the parking lot.

The path climbs first to the highway, then on to a display board in 0.25 mile, to the cemetery in less than 0.5 mile, and to the top of Mount Young (650 feet) at the end of a mile.

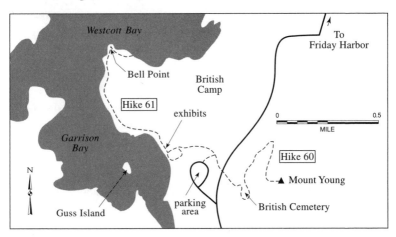

Garrison Bay and Haro Strait from Mount Young

A gravel path leads to the small, shady cemetery, where one civilian and seven members of the Royal Marine Light Infantry lie buried, most victims not of war but of accidental drownings in the surrounding sea.

The trail beyond the cemetery climbs sharply through madrona and maple trees with occasional glimpses of the Strait, ending in a series of unmarked spurs to rock outcrop views. A display at a formal overlook just below the summit identifies features in the area.

The best views, naturally, are found on the rounded top of the mountain. Wander or rest here where you will, framing pictures both west of the Strait and south to the Olympics from the rocky knolls carved by glaciers.

Note where you entered the open area atop the mountain so you can return the way you came.

61. BELL POINT

San Juan Island

Features	■	seashore
One way	■	0.5 mile
Elevation gain	■	none
Difficulty	■	easy
Open	■	all year
Map	■	San Juan Island National Historical Park brochure

An easy and pleasant forested trail winds along the shore of Garrison and Westcott Bays off Haro Strait to a pleasant picnic and rest stop at Bell Point.

English Camp from Bell Point Trail

Take the state ferry at the west end of North Cascades Highway 20 in Anacortes to San Juan Island. From the Friday Harbor ferry terminal, follow signs toward Roche Harbor, turning south toward British Camp, the northern half of the San Juan Island National Historical Park, at a T junction in about 9 miles. (See map on page 140.)

First, visit the garden and restored buildings of this nineteenth-century fort where the British faced a 66-man American army during a 12-year dispute over the arrest of an American settler who shot a British pig. A German kaiser finally settled the dispute by drawing the present Canada–U.S. border through Haro Strait.

(But don't think that American and British settlers were the first to live on this bay. Archeologists, digging in middens along the shore, have found evidence that Native Americans lived on the island 1,500 years ago.)

To find the trail to Bell Point, walk across the parade ground in front of the restored blockhouse, hospital, commissary, and farmhouse toward Garrison Bay, finding the trailhead to the right (north).

The path winds near the shore through a forest of madrona and Douglas fir to the point that separates Garrison and Westcott Bays and to views through the inlet into Haro Strait. For information about digging shellfish on park shores, check with rangers for locations, limits, and red tide warnings.

69. LIME KILN POINT STATE PARK

San Juan Island

Features	■	a lighthouse plus history, whales, and desert plants
One way	■	0.5 mile and less
Elevation gain	■	200 feet
Difficulty	■	easy
Open	■	manned in summer only
Map	■	State Park brochure

There are industrial stories here, strange plants, wooded trails, flashing lights, a horn moaning in the fog. But the real reason for stopping here is a chance to watch a pod of orca whales or a possible minke whale cruising near the shore.

From the Friday Harbor ferry terminal drive west on Spring Street,

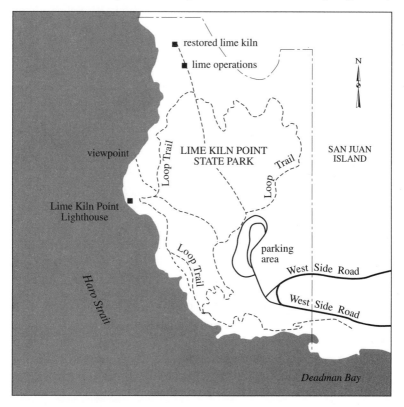

Cattle Point Lighthouse

bearing left on the San Juan Valley Road and left again onto Douglas Road then right on Bailer Hill Road which runs into the scenic West Side Road. Find the entrance to the park where the West Side Road jogs suddenly uphill to the right. Drive straight ahead to the parking area.

The whales, most commonly seen during the summer months, cruise the rocky shores along a trail in front of the lighthouse, feeding on salmon migrating to fresh water. Most seen are members of a resident pod of orcas that feed in the area all year. Outsiders sometimes join the parades. Often orcas can be seen from the West Side Road as you approach the entrance to the park. The minke whale travels alone and is more difficult to see.

None of the whales follow formal schedules. The Whale Museum in Friday Harbor keeps tab of whale sightings but again with no time schedules or current information on sightings.

The park offers tours of the lighthouse on Saturdays during the summer. The light that flashes every 10 seconds 50 feet above sea level is one of several lights on Haro Strait which divides the United States and Canada. The horn sounds its codes warnings whenever fog clouds the light.

The history here is defined by the lime kiln operation which began in 1860. One of the owners of the original lime operation shot the pig that started the Pig Wars, which lead to the military British–American standoff over the island boundaries. A German kaiser finally settled the dispute by drawing the line down the middle of Haro Strait.

Prickly-pear cactus, a tropical plant, grows along paths in the park. A loop trail lead to exhibits which define the plants, lime operations, marine mammals, and lighthouse functions.

63. SOUTH BEACH

San Juan Island

Features	■	beach, birds, great scenery
One way	■	about 1.5 miles
Elevation gain	■	negligible
Difficulty	■	easy
Open	■	all year
Map	■	San Juan Island National Historical Park brochure

Beaches, yes. The longest public beach on San Juan Island. With birds, vistas, and tide pools galore.

Take the state ferry from Anacortes to San Juan Island. From the Friday Harbor ferry terminal, drive west on Spring Street, turning south on Mullis Road. Continue on Argyle Avenue, and turn right and then south on Cattle Point Road to American Camp, the southern section of San Juan Island National Historical Park, a total of 6 miles from the ferry dock.

At the American Camp boundary, turn east on American Camp Road and south on Pickett's Lane to a beach spur road, picnic areas, and a parking area.

South Beach

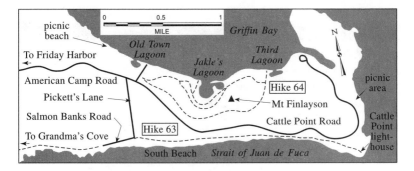

Your trail here is the beach and whatever way you want to walk: west over assorted headlands to Grandma's Cove, or east on sand beach (or path above the beach) toward Cattle Point.

Constant views over the Strait of Juan de Fuca of the Olympic Mountains, passing freighters, tugs with tows, cruising submarines, and, with luck, even orca whales. And at night? The glow of Victoria, British Columbia, and Port Angeles and Port Townsend, and the flashing lighthouse signals from Ediz Hook, Dungeness Spit, Smith Island, and Port Wilson on Admiralty Inlet.

And the birds? Shorebirds of every sort: gulls, terns, plovers, turnstones, and greater and lesser yellowlegs. And over the shoreland: hawks and bald eagles, certainly. Even turkey vultures, with their bald, red heads, seldom seen elsewhere in western Washington.

With tide pools, too, at low tide near the headlands to the west. Choose what your spirit moves you to, and spend whatever time you have.

64. JAKLE'S LAGOON

San Juan Island

Features	▪	forest, beach, and history
One way	▪	1-plus mile
Elevation gain	▪	100 feet
Difficulty	▪	moderate
Open	▪	all year
Map	▪	San Juan Island National Historical Park brochure

Two places here: the Jakle Farm, begun by an American soldier and his wife during the Pig War, now forest and wild meadowland, and

Bald eagle near Jackle's Lagoon

Jakle's Lagoon on Griffin Bay, which was used by Native Americans long before that "war." With the same marine life and birds now as then.

Take the state ferry from Anacortes to San Juan Island. From the Friday Harbor ferry terminal, drive west on Spring Street, turning south on Mullis Road. Continue on Argyle Avenue, and turn right and then south on Cattle Point Road to American Camp, the southern section of San Juan Island National Historical Park, a total of 6 miles from the ferry dock.

At the American Camp boundary, turn easterly on American Camp Road to the trailhead parking lot just beyond the junction with Pickett's Lane. Find the trail to the right of the parking lot. (See map on page 146.)

The nature trail through the abandoned farm drops downhill past numbered posts through a forest of Douglas fir, hemlock, maple, alder, and an occasional now-much-talked-of yew, all undergrown with flowers, ferns, mosses, and berries.

The posts mark natural features on a loop developed by the San Juan Horticulture Society. If the display box is empty, obtain a guide booklet at American Camp headquarters (on a spur road off Cattle Point Road where it turns east into American Camp Road).

In less than 1 mile, the trail turns uphill to the right and enters the meadow before turning back to the parking area.

To visit the beach, with views of both Mount Baker and Mount Rainier, take a spur trail left toward the water where the nature trail first levels out.

On the beach turn right to see Jakle's Lagoon in less than 0.5 mile. At the entrance to the lagoon, take time to examine the eroded bank. Note the thick layer of compressed seashell middens overgrown by sod. In the past, Native Americans ate the clams they harvested on the beach. Wonder, as you judge the thickness of the middens, how many years they camped and feasted here.

Take time, too, to wander the beach and pools in the shallow lagoon, noting the tracks of animals and birds that graze and feast here even now. And listen also for the cries of eagles nesting in the forests near the beach. Watch them soar away as you approach.

Take the trail from the lagoon back to the forest/nature loop to return to the parking lot.

65. ROSARIO HEAD / BOWMAN BAY

Fidalgo Island: Deception Pass State Park

Features	▪	pictures everywhere with tide pools, too
One way	▪	0.5 mile
Elevation gain	▪	about 100 feet
Difficulty	▪	moderate to steep
Open	▪	all year
Map	▪	Deception Pass State Park brochure

Beaches, yes. Tide pools, too. Panoramas on a sunny day that define everything that Northwest beauty is about.

From I-5, turn west on North Cascades Highway 20 at Exit 230 north of Mount Vernon and then turn south in about 12 miles to Deception Pass State Park.

Find both trails off Rosario Road, which branches west from Highway 20 north of the Deception Pass bridge and along the south end of Pass Lake. The road to Bowman Bay is the first one to the left; the road to Rosario Bay is the second road to the left.

Start from parking lots at either place, with the gentlest downhill walk from Rosario Head.

From the Rosario Bay parking area, walk south through the picnic

Tide pool at Bowman Bay

area between the boat dock on Bowman Bay and the tide pool rocks in Rosario Bay. (You may want to explore the pools at low tide here before proceeding toward Bowman Bay.)

Beyond the wood carving of the Maiden of Deception Pass (Kokwalalwood), follow the trail up the left (easiest) side of the rocky crest of Rosario Head to short trails with spectacular views east into Bowman Bay, south to Whidbey Island, and west to the San Juan Islands, Rosario Strait, and the Strait of Juan de Fuca.

Keep your camera and binoculars ready to check out the screams of oystercatchers and the chatter of kingfishers working the water and rocks below. Watch, too, for an occasional seal. And flowers in the spring.

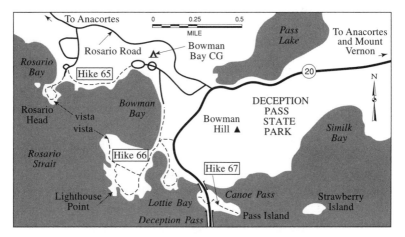

Warning: The bluff here, inviting as it is, drops steeply into rocks below. Do not let small children stray.

Once you've run out of film or have soaked up all the scenery your memory can hold, drop back down the bluff and take the broad path east toward Bowman Bay. Informal spur paths lead to the edge of the bluff before the trail drops to the campground on the bay.

Walk back the way you came unless you have arranged for someone to pick you up at the campground.

66. LIGHTHOUSE POINT / CANOE PASS

Fidalgo Island: Deception Pass State Park

Features	■	beaches, forest, views
One way	■	up to 0.75 mile
Elevation gain	■	100 feet
Difficulty	■	moderate
Open	■	all year
Map	■	Deception Pass State Park brochure

A single trail from a parking lot leads to two different places with two different views: One fork in the trail leads to views over a navigation light, the other to views of the spectacular Deception Pass bridge.

From I-5, turn west on North Cascades Highway 20 at Exit 230 (north of Mount Vernon) and then turn south in about 12 miles to Deception Pass State Park.

To reach the trail, turn right (west) off North Cascades Highway 20 just beyond Pass Lake (north of the Deception Pass bridge) onto Rosario Road and then left again on the first road to Bowman Bay. The trail starts from the parking lot on Bowman Bay before you enter Bowman Bay Campground. (See map on page 149.)

Find the path that leads to both trails near the shore of the bay beyond the boat ramp and fishing dock. At high tide, stay on the trail as it passes a small tidal marsh on the left (water birds nest here in the spring) and then switchbacks up and around the headland ahead of you before dropping back to water level on Lottie Bay and a strip of land connected to Lighthouse Point.

At low tide leave the trail, drop to the beach, and follow the shoreline to the strip of land.

To find Lighthouse Point, bear west along the narrow strip of land to a path up the south side of the island-like point.

The path leads to an exposed bluff with views above a navigation light over the pass and the straits, all with wildflowers in the spring. Do not attempt to climb to the unmanned light. It's not only prohibited but also dangerous.

The trail continues north past the light and ends at a point overlooking Bowman Bay and down on the place from which you started.

To reach the Canoe Pass vista point and its picture-perfect view of the bridge, return to the main trail at the east end of the flat strip of land or, if on the main trail from the parking lot, continue straight ahead.

On the main trail, take the first uphill fork to the vista point. The path loops back down to Lottie Bay.

Deception Pass bridge from Lighthouse Point

67. PASS ISLAND

Whidbey Island: Deception Pass State Park

Features	▪	rushing tides and a classic bridge
One way	▪	0.75 mile at most
Elevation gain	▪	about 100 feet
Difficulty	▪	steep and no formal trails
Open	▪	all year
Map	▪	Deception Pass State Park brochure

Explore a ship of rock set in a speeding tidal stream at the end of one of the most spectacular bridges in the state.

From I-5, turn west on North Cascades highway 20 at exit 230 (north of Mount Vernon) and then turn south in about 12 miles to Deception Pass State Park. (See map on page 149.)

Find a small parking area on the left atop Pass Island where the highway curves to cross the Deception Pass bridge. (If you miss it, drive across the bridge, turn back at the parking lot at the south end, and return to the small Pass Island area just beyond a rock outcrop at the north end of the bridge.)

You'll find no formal trails here, but well-used routes lead east and west. Drop from a rock outcrop east of the parking area and pick paths to the right that cross under the bridge to views back at the bridge and out over the west end of the pass. Drop down the rocky slope straight ahead to find paths leading to fishing spots at the eastern end of the island.

The views, the rushing tides, and an unusual mixture of plants make any exploration here rewarding. Each path leads to different views of the impressive bridge and the other islands around it. The tides rush through the pass from 9 to 14 knots—among the fastest currents near this juncture of Sound and Strait. Looking down, the rushing tide often seems to transform the island into a speeding ship.

Plants from the seashore mix with those of the mountains and others more commonly seen east of the mountains, making careful examination of what you see worthwhile.

One caution: No matter what you do, use care in selecting your route. Follow well-worn paths only. The slopes here are very steep. Some paths quickly disappear. All can be slippery when wet. Not for uncontrolled children, the skittish, or the unprepared. Good shoes are a must. Care is essential.

Aerial view of Deception Pass and Pass Island

68. SAND DUNE TRAIL

Whidbey Island: Deception Pass State Park

Features	■	wetlands, dunes, beach, forest
One way	■	a short 1-mile loop
Elevation gain	■	none
Difficulty	■	easy
Open	■	all year
Map	■	Deception Pass State Park brochure

A sampler here, on a small scale, of all the changes in Nature—in the plants, animals, and birds—that take place, one grain of sand at a time, in every dune system up and down the coast.

Turn west on North Cascades Highway 20 at Exit 230 (north of Mount Vernon) and then turn south in about 12 miles to Deception Pass State Park.

Storm-twisted trees along Sand Dune Trail

From the end of the main entrance road to Deception Pass State Park, off Highway 20 south of the Deception Pass bridge, turn left on the main park road and continue to the right along the northern shore of Cranberry Lake to the large parking area near the beach.

Find the Sand Dune Trail beyond the concession stand near Cranberry Lake south of the parking lot. A mural here describes the ever-changing ecological contrasts seen along the loop. Other displays define natural features along the way.

The paved path first heads into trees away from the hubbub of the beach and, except for the occasional sounds of jets, into a more silent world of wind, waves, and birds. Find picnic tables hidden in the trees.

The first spur trail to the left leads to a viewing platform over-looking a marsh bordering Cranberry Lake. The shallows here are swamped with willows, skunk cabbages, and cattails. Seagulls are joined by marsh birds, hawks, and bald eagles now and then.

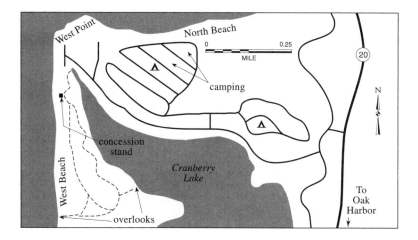

Back on the forest section of the trail, note the changing procession of plants. In the forest, established conifers, rhododendrons, and even scraggly looking yews stand amid bracken ferns and struggling flowers.

As the path circles toward the beach through a short, moist plain behind the low row of dunes, stunted coast pines, salal, and evergreen huckleberry give way to grasses and scattered beach-adapted lupine, strawberries, tansy, and the like. And, finally, on the dunes themselves, only clumps of grass stabilize the sand.

A spur trail leads through the dunes to another overlook with views over Rosario Strait and the Strait of Juan de Fuca. A return trail trail crosses a sparsely vegetated plain between the forest and the dunes.

69. ANACORTES BEAVER POND

Fidalgo Island

Features ▪	beaver pond and dams
One way ▪	0.75 mile
Elevation gain ▪	none
Difficulty ▪	easy
Open ▪	all year
Map ▪	Trail Guide to Anacortes Community Forest Land

Active beaver ponds at a city's edge? In 2,200 acres of forests, wetlands, lakes, and mountaintops in a "city" forest? Believe it. And try a sample here.

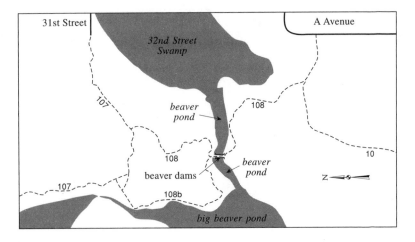

From I-5, turn west to Anacortes on North Cascades Highway 20 (north of Mount Vernon) and follow street signs in the center of town to 12th Street, the road to the Anacortes ferry terminal. From 12th Street, turn left (south) onto D Avenue and right (west) onto 31st Street, driving to the end of the short residential street. (Don't block driveways, please.)

Find the trail off the end of the street where the forest begins.

The path starts out through dense undergrowth of salal and salmon-berries and brown thickets of young trees, then enters a more mature forest with open sword fern groves and occasional explosions of lush yellow skunk cabbages in the spring.

At the first junction, follow Trail 108 to the left (signs here are posted horse-high in trees), and when you cross the first stream stop. Yes, stop.

On your left, a cattail and skunk cabbage swamp where ducks explode as you approach. And on your right—look twice—a beaver dam. An old beaver dam, overgrown with grass, yes, but—if you look a second time—you'll see it patched here and there with fresh sticks in newly eroded spots.

Turn back at the bridge and take Trail 108b to explore above the dam. Short way paths here lead to the top of the dam and closer views of the beavers' engineering skills. And note the tracks of deer and other creatures in muddy spots.

For fuller views of the marsh behind the dam, explore way paths off Trail 108b for about 0.25 mile. Here, dead trees killed by rising

Beaver Pond Trail

water in the pond and gnawed stumps of small trees cut and carted off by beavers attest to the beavers' work.

And no, you'll probably see no beavers here, although you may now and then hear an explosive splash, a signal that your presence is now known. Beavers do most of their work at night.

Return to the dam to continue on Trail 108 through more scattered old-growth cedar and Douglas fir. The trail ends at A Avenue on an old road to a nearby dump. Walk back to your car the way you came or arrange to be picked up. Bicycles and motorcycles are permitted on some of the many other trails.

70. WHISTLE LAKE

Fidalgo Island

Features ■	forest and lake
One way ■	0.75 mile
Elevation gain ■	slight
Difficulty ■	easy
Open ■	all year
Map ■	Trail Guide to Anacortes Community Forest Land

Hike past several giant, fire-scarred Douglas fir and great, old cedar trees that survived logging at the turn of the century to a popular lake in the 2,200-acre Anacortes Community Forest.

From I-5, turn west toward Anacortes on North Cascades Highway 20 (north of Mount Vernon) and turn left in Anacortes on Commercial Avenue at the first T intersection as you enter town. Turn quickly left onto Fidalgo and left again at St. Mary's Catholic Church. Turn right on Hillcrest and right again on Whistle Lake Road. Jog left at the end of that road and then right, following signs downhill to a parking area and trailhead, about 1.75 miles from the T intersection.

Find Gerry Wallrath Trail straight ahead at a gate off the parking area. Wallrath was an early supporter of efforts to preserve these forests for the city and left his estate to support the maintenance and development of the trail system.

You can't get lost here. Stay on the main trail, which was once a service road for what was then the city's water system. The several ancient trees define what the forest here once was. The second-growth demonstrates what it has yet to achieve before it equals that grandeur.

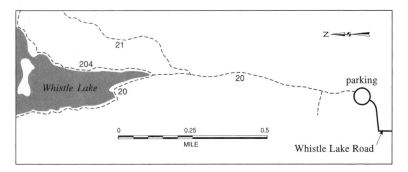

And the mix of the two illustrates the continuity of earlier selective logging techniques. In such forests, today's great old trees were already standing when the first trees were cut. And if today's older trees were to be logged, the remaining younger trees would already be in place to fill their roles.

The trail ends at the lakeshore. Fishing, swimming, and rafting here. Experienced swimmers with local knowledge hike up the right side of the lake about 0.5 mile on Trail 204 to a narrow passage between the shoreline and a small island. Young people swim to the island where they climb a bluff and dive into the lake.

And watch for birds. Pileated woodpeckers, osprey, bald eagles, and wood ducks are common here.

Whistle Lake

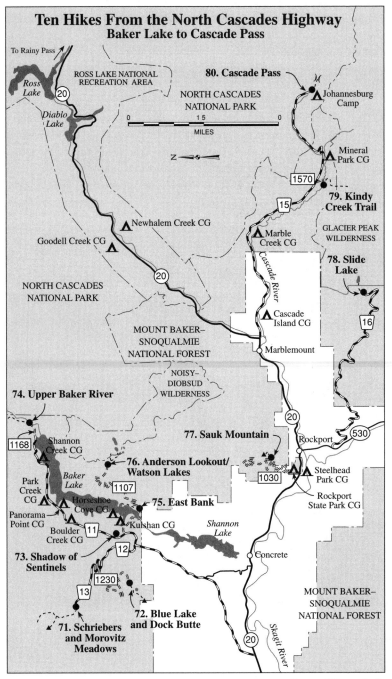

Ten Hikes From the North Cascades Highway
Baker Lake to Cascade Pass

To Rainy Pass

Ross Lake

ROSS LAKE NATIONAL RECREATION AREA

80. Cascade Pass

NORTH CASCADES NATIONAL PARK

Johannesburg Camp

Diablo Lake

Z

0   1 5   0
MILES

Mineral Park CG

1570

15

79. Kindy Creek Trail

Newhalem Creek CG

Marble Creek CG

GLACIER PEAK WILDERNESS

Goodell Creek CG

78. Slide Lake

20

16

NORTH CASCADES NATIONAL PARK

Cascade Island CG

MOUNT BAKER– SNOQUALMIE NATIONAL FOREST

Marblemount

NOISY– DIOBSUD WILDERNESS

74. Upper Baker River

77. Sauk Mountain

Rockport

530

1168

Shannon Creek CG

Baker Lake

76. Anderson Lookout/ Watson Lakes

1030

Steelhead Park CG

Park Creek CG

1107

75. East Bank

Rockport State Park CG

Panorama Point CG

Horseshoe Cove CG

Kulshan CG

Shannon Lake

Boulder Creek CG

11

73. Shadow of Sentinels

12

Concrete

MOUNT BAKER– SNOQUALMIE NATIONAL FOREST

1230

13

72. Blue Lake and Dock Butte

Skagit River

71. Schriebers and Morovitz Meadows

20

Lower Watson Lake

TEN
HIKES FROM THE
NORTH CASCADES
HIGHWAY

BAKER LAKE TO CASCADE PASS

Explore the edge of wildness here on trails that sample the protected Mount Baker National Recreation Area, the North Cascades National Park, the Noisy–Diobsud Wilderness, and the Glacier Peak Wilderness.

In the Mount Baker National Recreation Area explore the glorious alpine **Schriebers and Morovitz Meadows** (Hike 71) commanded by Mount Baker. Along the **Upper Baker River** (Hike 74) explore a corner of the North Cascades wilderness. And find **Anderson Butte and Watson Lakes** (Hike 76) just inside the Noisy–Diobsud Wilderness. And then hike up to **Cascade Pass** (Hike 80) in the North Cascade National Park, perhaps the most spectacular of them all. And that's not to forget **Dock Butte, Sauk Mountain,** or **Kindy Creek.**

For information on campgrounds nearby, see Appendix 1, Campgrounds. For current reports on trail and road conditions contact the Mount Baker Ranger Station or see the Mount Baker–Snoqualmie National Forest website (see Appendix 2).

71. SCHRIEBERS AND MOROVITZ MEADOWS

Features	■	mountains and meadows
One way	■	2.5 miles
Elevation gain	■	400 feet
Difficulty	■	steep in places
Open	■	summer
Map	■	Green Trails 45

From one great meadow to another, with Mount Baker watching all the way, first through trees and then majestically down open, flowered slopes.

From I-5 north of Mount Vernon, turn east at Exit 230 onto North Cascades Highway 20. About 14.5 miles east of Sedro Woolley, turn north onto Baker Lake Road and reach the boundary of Mount Baker–Snoqualmie National Forest (it's signed) in about 12 miles.

To find the trail, turn left (west) off Baker Lake Road just inside the forest boundary onto Forest Road 12 and then, in 3.5 miles, onto Forest Road 13. Find the trailhead in 5 more miles off a well-developed parking area, to the left, beside the toilets.

The first mile of the trail to Schriebers Meadow wanders through increasingly open timber and past occasional small ponds, each with its own reflected glimpse of Mount Baker. Other clearings and small patches of trees with still more ponds and sinkholes everywhere.

(Swarms of mosquitoes here most summers, but bugless in the fall when the meadows turn rich with berries and color.)

At the end of the mile, the trail passes the site of a former shelter

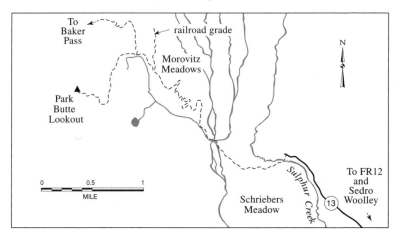

Morovitz Meadows and Mount Baker

and crosses streams from Easton Glacier before a steep switchback climb to the more open Morovitz Meadows at 4,700 feet, with still more views and places begging to be explored.

At the meadows, it is impossible to say which way to turn. One ridge may look down on a whole city of marmots, another out on a flower slope. The next may feature wind-sculptured trees. Another, snarls of rock. But over all of them, no matter which you choose, your host, proud and stately Mount Baker.

Other trails—all uphill—continue on to the railroad grade (4,900 feet), Baker Pass (5,000 feet), and Park Butte Lookout (5,400 feet). And each is worth the trip.

72. BLUE LAKE AND DOCK BUTTE

Features	■	lake, meadows, mountain views
One way	■	Blue Lake, 0.75 mile; Dock Butte, 1 mile
Elevation gain	■	Blue Lake, 100 feet; Dock Butte, 700 feet
Difficulty	■	steep in places
Open	■	summer
Map	■	Green Trails 45

Two destinations and two trails here, really. Each worth a visit all its own. But both are so closely linked that to hike to one without visiting the other would be a waste of effort.

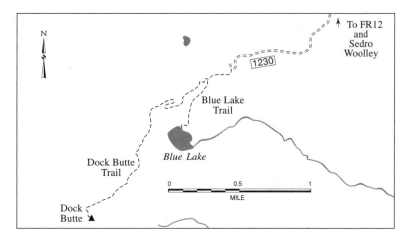

From I-5 north of Mount Vernon, turn east at Exit 230 onto North Cascades Highway 20. About 14.5 miles east of Sedro Woolley, turn north onto Baker Lake Road and reach the boundary of Mount Baker–Snoqualmie National Forest (it's signed) in about 12 miles.

To find the trail, turn left (west) off Baker Lake Road just inside the forest boundary onto Forest Road 12. In 7 miles, turn left onto Forest Road 1230, driving another 4 miles to the end of the road (with views of Baker, Shuksan, Blum, and other North Cascades peaks in the last 3 miles).

At the end of the road, the trail climbs a slight ridge less than 0.5 mile to a junction: Dock Butte Trail to the right, Blue Lake Trail to the left. The Dock Butte Trail climbs steadily up a series of switchbacks with increasing views toward Mount Baker, reaching an open meadow at about 4,700 feet—with flowers in the summer, colors in the fall—atop a beautiful alpine plateau.

Follow the trail south past pleasant pools, gray outcrops of rock, overgrown mine prospects, weathered trees, and camping spots. Views swing here from the Twin Sisters in the east to Baker and Shuksan, up the Baker River valley to the Pickets, and westward to Blum, Hagan, and Bacon.

Wander here certainly before returning to the lake. And, if you choose, climb a rugged and very steep path another 0.5 mile and up another 500 feet to the top of the pointed butte and the former Dock Butte lookout site at 5,200 feet. Not for the queasy. Add Mount Rainier here to your list of peaks.

On the way down, turn right downhill at the trail junction to visit Blue Lake. The soggy path drops downhill through timber to a 13-acre

Mount Baker from Dock Butte

lake at 4,000 feet. Talus slopes rise at the far end, meadows surround the rest.

73. SHADOW OF SENTINELS

Features ▪	old-growth forest
One way ▪	0.5-mile loop
Elevation gain ▪	none
Difficulty ▪	easy (wheelchair trail)
Open ▪	spring to winter
Map ▪	Green Trails 46

Find here all the reasons ever needed for preserving what's left of old-growth forests in western Washington. All from one lush, short, and easy trail.

Shadow of Sentinels Nature Trail

From I-5 north of Mount Vernon, turn east at Exit 230 onto North Cascades Highway 20. About 14.5 miles east of Sedro Woolley, turn north onto Baker Lake–Grandy Lake Road (or the road to Baker Lake, depending on the sign you read) and reach the boundary of Mount Baker–Snoqualmie National Forest (it's signed) in about 12 miles.

From the boundary, continue on Baker Lake–Grandy Lake Road (now Forest Road 11) about 3.5 miles, finding the nature trail on the right about 0.75 mile beyond the Koma Kulshan Guard Station.

You'll find the best of every ancient forest here on this one short loop. Huge Douglas firs and hemlocks, some more than 600 years old, tower high above a still-evolving, multilayered canopy of younger trees that rise over, and from, other rotting giants toppled by time and winds.

Not a trail to rush through, no, for this old forest is more than trees. Admire the mosses, the variety of ferns, the scraps of lichens on the trail, and the change of wildflowers (a new display for every week). And listen to the croak of frogs, the trill of wrens, the thrush's scale of single notes, the drum of woodpeckers on rotting snags, and even the robin's call.

Bring your camera, binoculars, bird and flower books, for you'll find here—if you take the time to look—what you'll find in most west-slope,

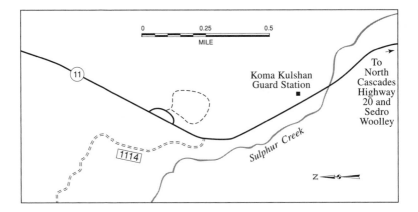

old-growth forests everywhere, assuring you, in saying that, that every forest grove is different and that having seen one you've not seen all. An excellent sample here. No more.

74. UPPER BAKER RIVER

Features	■	river and forest
One way	■	1.5 miles or less
Elevation gain	■	200 feet
Difficulty	■	moderate
Open	■	spring to fall
Map	■	Green Trails 14

A mountain river here, wild, fresh, and untrammeled, flowing from the North Cascades into Baker Lake with views of more than just Mount Baker.

From I-5 north of Mount Vernon, turn east at Exit 230 onto North Cascades Highway 20. About 14.5 miles east of Sedro Woolley, turn north onto Baker Lake–Grandy Lake Road (or the road to Baker Lake, depending on the sign you read) and reach the boundary of Mount Baker–Snoqualmie National Forest (it's signed) in about 12 miles.

From the boundary, continue on Baker Lake–Grandy Lake Road (now Forest Road 11) to its end, with views of Mount Baker all along the way, and then turn left on Spur Road 1168 with a parking lot and trailhead at its end, about 14.5 miles from the boundary.

The trail starts down a long-abandoned logging spur away from the river, off the upstream side of the parking lot. In less than 0.25 mile,

Upper Baker River

the spur ends and the trail enters a cluster of grand old cedar trees and then winds around huge boulders, under arches of moss-draped vine maples and across several short log bridges.

Watch for indications of a beaver pond through the trees and undergrowth on your left. Old alders stand by themselves in the middle of the water. No approach to the ponds.

Take time to walk the suspension bridge that crosses the river to a horse trail that ends at the East Bank Trail 75. Then visit every cove along the river and explore every sandbar and gravel bar. Note, too, how the river continues to shape the valley as it sweeps back and forth on an ever-changing course, adding shoreline here, destroying it there.

Wild salmon once spawned here. Now, returning salmon have to be trucked in from Concrete to spawning grounds above the dam.

In about a mile, the trail climbs around a rocky point and then drops away from the river across a brushy flat, reaching the boundary of North Cascades National Park at 1.75 miles.

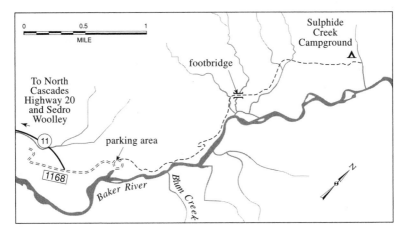

The trail ends in another 0.75 mile at a small campground on Sulphide Creek. Backcountry permits are required for camping there.

75. EAST BANK

Features	■	forest, lake, history
One way	■	2 miles
Elevation loss	■	300 feet
Difficulty	■	moderate
Open	■	spring to winter
Map	■	Green Trails 46

First, walk through a forest logged selectively ninety years ago. It is as rich now as it was then. Next, follow a spur path to Baker Lake and an explosive view of the lake's namesake peak.

From I-5 north of Mount Vernon, turn east at Exit 230 onto North Cascades Highway 20. About 14.5 miles east of Sedro Woolley, turn north onto Baker Lake–Grandy Lake Road (or the road to Baker Lake, depending on the sign you read) and reach the boundary of Mount Baker–Snoqualmie National Forest (it's signed) in about 12 miles.

Continue north on what has now become Forest Road 11. Turn right onto Forest Road 1106 to cross the top of Upper Baker Dam, and then follow Forest Road 1107 around to the left (toward Anderson Lookout/Watson Lakes, Hike 76).

In little more than 0.5 mile find a parking strip on the left and the East Bank beginning of the 14-mile trail along the lake to the Baker River (see Hike 74).

Mount Baker reflected in Baker Lake

The path drops immediately into new forest and then across three little creeks before leveling out in a much older forest. Note here the huge old stumps hand-logged by men who stood on springboards jammed into the side of the tree.

Note also that the forest here is probably as open now as it was when the original trees were first cut down. Most of the larger trees here now, no doubt, were well established when the much larger trees were

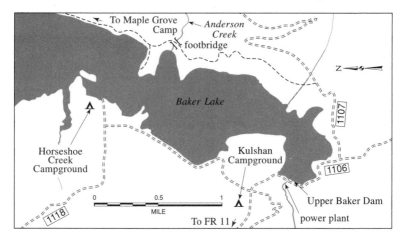

felled. Loggers then did not cut every tree in sight but only those they sent to the mill. (Some of the big Douglas fir here today could never have attained their present size in just ninety years.)

The path, which now sometimes goes up while seeming to go down, climbs over the toe of a ridge, drops, and climbs again before dropping to a large log bridge over noisy Anderson Creek.

Views now of Mount Baker from a beach on a small cove and sand spit at the end of a short unmarked path downhill to the left at the start of the bridge.

Beyond the bridge in 0.5 mile more or less, take a more developed spur trail to the left, which drops for 0.25 mile down a neck of land to the lake with even better views.

Stop here or return to the main trail and hike on to Maple Grove Camp, largely for fishermen, boaters, and horseback riders. Or on to the Baker River bridge (see Upper Baker River, Hike 74).

76. ANDERSON LOOKOUT / WATSON LAKES

Features	▪	mountain lakes and a lookout, too
One way	▪	3.5 miles
Elevation gain	▪	500 to 1,200 feet
Difficulty	▪	steep to very steep
Open	▪	summer
Map	▪	Green Trails 46

Two clusters of alpine lakes at 4,500 feet in spectacular meadow country plus an even higher (5,400 feet) former lookout site with views almost everywhere, all from the end of a high, scenic forest road.

From I-5 north of Mount Vernon, turn east at Exit 230 onto North Cascades Highway 20. About 14.5 miles east of Sedro Woolley, turn north onto Baker Lake–Grandy Lake Road (or the road to Baker Lake, depending on the sign you read) and reach the boundary of Mount Baker–Snoqualmie National Forest (it's signed) in about 12 miles.

Continue north on what has now become Forest Road 11, turn right onto Forest Road 1106, cross the top of Upper Baker Dam, and then follow Forest Road 1107 about 9-plus miles, turning left on Spur Road 1107-022 to trailhead parking.

The trail to both clusters of lakes and the lookout starts sharply from the parking area, climbing briskly the first mile to the junction with Anderson Butte Trail. It's another long 0.5 mile to the junction

Watson Lakes

with Watson Lakes Trail, and a final 0.5 plus mile to Anderson Lakes.

From the main trail, the path to the lookout site on Anderson Butte switchbacks up persistently and often steeply 700 feet in 0.5 mile to a boulder outcrop on the edge of the Noisy–Diobsud Wilderness, with awesome views of Mounts Baker and Shuksan and other Cascade peaks to the south. No views of the lakes.

Returning to the main trail, take the path to Watson Lakes that climbs steeply uphill to the left over a ridge into the Noisy–Diobsud Wilderness before dropping to the lakes. Views of both from a steep meadow before you reach the lakes. (A trail along the left side of the first lake leads to the second.)

The main trail continues to the first of the Anderson Lakes and drops gradually through meadows from the Watson Lakes turnoff.

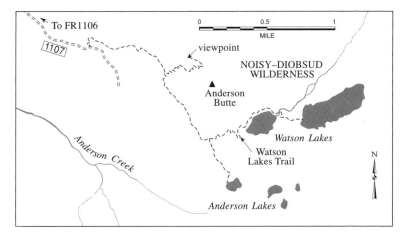

Bears right at the first lake for a breathtaking look of Mount Baker from a pretty meadow just across the creek. No formal trail to two other lakes that lie about 500 feet higher atop the ridge to the left.

Camping at Watson Lakes near the first lake or on meadows between the two lakes. Camping also near Anderson Lake.

Spend a day at either one, or a weekend at both.

77. SAUK MOUNTAIN

Features ■	steep meadows and grand vistas
One way ■	2-plus miles
Elevation gain ■	1,200 feet
Difficulty ■	steep
Open ■	summer
Map ■	Green Trails 46

Great views of the Sauk, Skagit, and Cascade River valleys from a zigzag forest road that leads to the trail parking lot and then to a spectacle of peaks from an old lookout site at 5,537 feet, at the end of an exciting trail.

From I-5 north of Mount Vernon, turn east at Exit 230 onto North Cascades Highway 20 and drive to Concrete. In about another 10 miles, turn north (left) on easy-to-miss Forest Road 1030 along the western boundary of Rockport State Park (about 1.5 miles west of the junction of Highways 20 and 530 in Rockport).

Forest Road 1030 switchbacks a low-gear 7 miles to a junction on

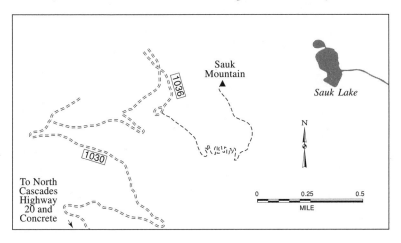

the right with short Spur Road 1036. Turn right to turnaround parking with the grand overlook in a few hundred yards at the end of the spur.

Find the trail to the top of Sauk Mountain off the east side of the parking area. It drops slightly at the start but then begins a steady switchback climb across steep meadows to the ridge top and lookout site.

No one seems to agree on the number of switchbacks on this trail. Some say twenty-six, others twenty-eight, and still others twenty-nine. But the truth is, it doesn't really matter. First, because most of them are short, and second, because the demanding, ever-changing views and spectacular flower meadows make counting impossible anyway.

At the ridge, a spur path branches right and drops down, about as far as you have climbed, to Sauk Lake. Most hikers pass up the opportunity and continue ahead to the lookout site in a less steep and long 0.5 mile to fantastic views of Glacier Peak; Mounts Baker, Shuksan, Whitehorse, White Chuck, and Pugh; and, on clear days, Mount Rainier, Puget Sound, and the San Juan Islands.

A warning: Use care here. Do not shortcut switchbacks or dislodge rocks. And warn those who do that they are endangering the lives of those on the trail below them.

Skagit River from Sauk Mountain Trail

78. SLIDE LAKE

Features	■	forest and lake with supporting ponds
One way	■	1.25 miles
Elevation gain	■	300 feet
Difficulty	■	moderate
Open	■	summer
Map	■	Green Trails 79

Surprising ponds and a spectacular lake, tucked in a mountain bowl at the end of a short trail filled with moss-covered boulders and other surprises.

From I-5 north of Mount Vernon, turn east at Exit 230 onto North Cascades Highway 20 and drive to Rockport. From Rockport drive south on Rockport–Darrington Highway 530, and turn east (left) in 1.9 miles onto Illabot Creek Forest Road 16. Drive 20 miles to the Otter Creek trailhead.

The path to Slide Lake wanders through a cool, shady tumble of old boulders topped with huge, ancient hemlocks. Don't hurry. Nature worked a long time to create this scene, so soak up all of the visual surprises as you go. Forest flowers, huckleberries, salmonberries, and gooseberries in season.

The trail enters the Glacier Peak Wilderness at the end of a mile, skirts several ponds, and reaches the main lake (3,300 feet), with the best views just 0.25 mile farther.

Camp and picnic places at the end of the trail along with views up

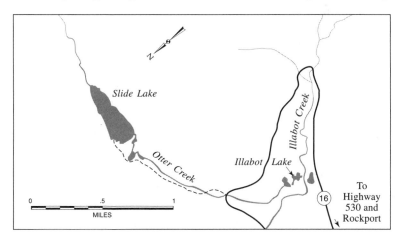

Slide Lake

at Snowking Mountain. Treat the area with care: It has been heavily used over time, as you can see. Without your consideration it could still be destroyed.

79. KINDY CREEK TRAIL

Features ■	rich forest
One way ■	1-plus mile
Elevation gain ■	about 200 feet
Difficulty ■	moderate
Open ■	summer
Map ■	trail not shown on Forest Service or Green Trails maps

A wild, grand grove of ancient hemlock, cedar, and Douglas fir on an unmarked trail that you, at least, will not forget. Most of the time, you'll be the only hiker (or hikers) there.

From I-5 north of Mount Vernon, turn east at Exit 230 onto North Cascades Highway 20 and continue to Marblemount. From Marblemount, continue east across the Skagit River on Cascade River Road 15.

About 6 miles beyond Marble Creek Campground, turn sharply south (right) just beyond the 13-mile marker onto Forest Road 1570.

(Watch for a wide turnout on the left side of the road where big trucks swing wide off the spur.)

Follow Forest Road 1570 downhill, keeping straight ahead at the first fork, crossing the Cascade River in about 1.6 miles, and turning left on the far side of the bridge.

In about 0.3 mile, turn left onto Forest Road 1571, driving to the end of the road at a rotting bridge across Kindy Creek.

Walk across the bridge over this startling, clear creek and follow an old logging track to a wide point where the road once turned up-hill. (Avoid the inviting game trails that climb steeply across sandy slopes to your right.)

The old road ends and the real Kindy Creek Trail begins at an unused trail board in another 100 yards or less.

The trail, now a pleasant path, climbs gradually back toward Kindy Creek through everything you'd expect to see in an open, untouched forest, with towering trees up to 8 feet in diameter.

As spring and summer pass: star flowers and Queen's cup, through bunchberries and pipsissewas, to huckleberries and even salal amid

Tall trees on Kindy Creek Trail

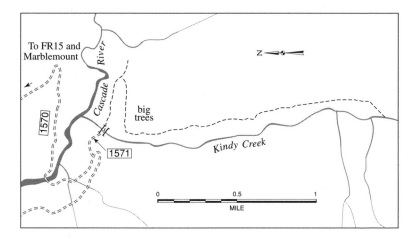

colored vine maples into the fall. The path crests at about 1,500 feet before dropping down and ending in a washout on Kindy Creek, well above the place you started. Return the way you came, taking time to note all the beauties you may have missed.

80. CASCADE PASS

Features ▪	endless mountain spectacles
One way ▪	3.75 miles
Elevation gain ▪	1,800 feet
Difficulty ▪	steep
Open ▪	midsummer
Map ▪	Green Trails 80

The queen of all short Cascade mountain hikes. Longer, yes, than most of the others listed here. But you'll forget the added effort in the spectacle of glaciers, peaks, flowers, and rugged mountains that surround you.

From I-5 north of Mount Vernon, turn east at Exit 230 onto North Cascades Highway 20 and continue to Marblemount. Continue east across the Skagit River on Cascade River Road 15 and drive 25 miles to a parking area at the end of the road in North Cascades National Park.

The grandeur here begins before you even leave your car at 3,600 feet. From just the parking area: glaciers on Johannesburg Mountain to the southwest and Cascade Pass above you to the east.

The trail to Cascade Pass from the parking lot switchbacks very gradually through trees, topping out at last on a long traverse up to

Eldorado Peak, left, and Boston Basin, right, from small tarn near Cascade Pass

the pass (5,400 feet) across alpine meadows. Panoramas, yes, but closer up, paintbrush, monkey flower, penstemon, and whole hillsides of red columbine, just to list the obvious flowers.

At the pass, whistling marmots, certainly. Pikas scurrying in the rocks. But most of all, glaciers everywhere with avalanches crashing from their hanging cliffs of ice.

And views to the east out over the Stehekin Valley.

If you have time, walk the switchback path just beyond the crest uphill to the left toward Sahale Arm for even more exciting vistas. Another mile and 800 feet will take you to a ridge overlooking Doubtful Lake and still broader views of the towering peaks around you.

No camping permitted at the pass, and hikers are urged to stay on the trail. Heavy use here in the past almost destroyed this area for good.

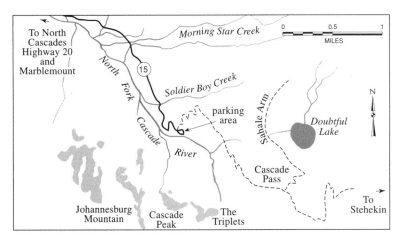

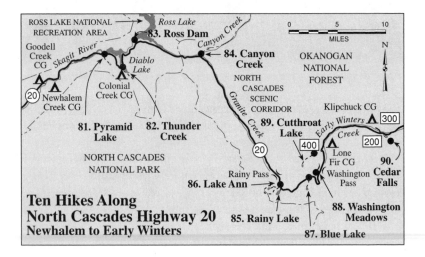

ROSS LAKE NATIONAL
RECREATION AREA

Ross Lake

83. Ross Dam

Canyon Creek

Goodell
Creek
CG

Skagit River

*Diablo
Lake*

0   5   10
MILES

N

**84. Canyon
Creek**

OKANOGAN
NATIONAL
FOREST

20 Newhalem
Creek CG

Colonial
Creek CG

NORTH
CASCADES
SCENIC
CORRIDOR

Klipchuck CG

Early Winters 300

**81. Pyramid
Lake**

**82. Thunder
Creek**

Granite Creek

**89. Cutthroat
Lake**

Creek

200

NORTH CASCADES
NATIONAL PARK

20

400

Lone
Fir CG

**90.
Cedar
Falls**

Rainy Pass

86. Lake Ann

Washington
Pass

**Ten Hikes Along
North Cascades Highway 20**
Newhalem to Early Winters

85. Rainy Lake

**88. Washington
Meadows**

87. Blue Lake

Azurite Peak and Grasshopper Pass from the Pacific Crest Trail near Tatie Peak

TEN

HIKES ALONG NORTH CASCADES HIGHWAY

NEWHALEM TO EARLY WINTERS

East of the Cascades see the high mountain beauty of North Cascades National Park, closed in the winter but open to hosts of wildflowers and high blue lakes from spring to fall.

Hike rich forest trails near a campground on **Thunder Creek** (Hike 82). Find vast panoramas above a lush flower meadow at **Washington Pass** (Hike 88). Walk a mile to **Rainy Lake** (Hike 85) or 2 miles to **Lake Ann** (Hike 86) or see both on a 7.4-mile loop. Or stand in the mist of a roaring torrent at **Cedar Falls** (Hike 90).

For information on campgrounds nearby, see Appendix 1, Campgrounds. For current information on trail and road conditions contact the North Cascades National Park, Methow Valley Ranger District, or see Okanogan–Wenatchee National Forest website (see Appendix 2).

81. PYRAMID LAKE

Features	▪	forest and tiny lake
One way	▪	a long 2 miles
Elevation gain	▪	1,500 feet
Difficulty	▪	very steep
Open	▪	summer
Map	▪	Green Trails 48

Peculiarly, this is a very popular trail. You'll find smiling adults and children working their way up and down it almost any day and time of day all summer long. But if you've hiked other trails almost anywhere in this region, you'll have to wonder why.

First, it's steep beyond belief. The lake at the end is almost small enough to spit across. And the forest, for the first third at least, is the scrawniest and most unattractive in this entire book.

So why the many who struggle here? Who knows. You'll have to hike and judge it for yourself.

From I-5 north of Mount Vernon, turn east at Exit 230 onto North Cascades Highway 20 and continue through Marblemount to the Seattle City Light community of Newhalem.

Find the trail to the lake about 6.5 miles east of Newhalem (3.4 miles west of Colonial Creek Campground), with parking on the north (lake) side of the highway. The trail is uphill across the road in a gully.

The rocky path grinds up through an old burn now grown with scrawny lodgepole pine, past an occasional old Douglas fir scarred, but not destroyed, by fire.

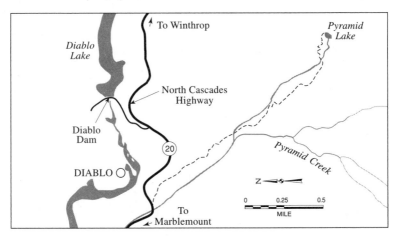

After maybe a 700-foot gain in elevation and a glimpse of Pyramid Peak through the trees, the path wanders briefly through a grove of old cedars and fir before climbing again in short, steep spurts over roots and rocks—up 100 feet here and 200 feet there—through still more small groves (note occasional old blazes on the trees) until—voila!—at 2,600 feet, the lake! A pond! A puddle! The end! With barely a place to sit and rest. With a glimpse—no more—of Pyramid Peak above the trees.

All may not be lost, however. And the word is "may." Sundews, small insect-eating plants, have been noted on logs floating in this small pond. And if you find one, look but leave it be. Give others the chance to find the plant.

And oh, yes. Return the way you came, finding it just as steep going down as it was when you struggled up.

Pyramid Peak from Pyramid Lake

82. THUNDER CREEK

Features	▪	rich forest, flowers, creek
One way	▪	2 miles or less
Elevation gain	▪	300 feet
Difficulty	▪	easy to moderate
Open	▪	summer
Map	▪	Green Trails 48

From one path here, two destinations: a pleasant, level river walk up Thunder Creek and a generous sample of a mountain forest on the Thunder Woods Nature Trail. Both are worth the trip.

From I-5 north of Mount Vernon, turn east at Exit 230 onto North Cascades Highway 20 and continue to Marblemount. Then drive north 24 miles to Colonial Creek Campground on Thunder Arm in North Cascades National Park.

Find the start of both these hikes behind the amphitheater at the far end of the loop in the southern, upriver side of the campground.

Thunder Woods Nature Trail. Find the mile-long trail uphill at a display sign about 0.25 mile from the amphitheater. The path here loops up through almost every type of natural setting to be found in old-growth, unlogged forests in this park: ancient cedars straddle boulders, towering Douglas firs perch on stilts above the rotting logs they sprouted on, and old giants sprawl across the forest floor, their upended root fans decked with ferns, while the rotting trunks of other fallen giants sprout seedling trees.

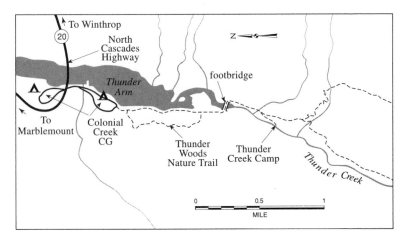

Thunder Creek Trail

The trail, like all good forest trails, climbs here, drops there, struggles over roots and rocks and even crosses a slope of scree. Most often, though, it winds gently through a silence that pervades ancient forests everywhere.

After climbing about 300 feet past all the numbered stations explained in the park brochure, the path drops to the main trail: turn left to camp, or right down Thunder Arm again.

Thunder Arm Trail. From the campground, this trail winds above Thunder Arm more than 0.75 mile and then crosses a suspension bridge over Thunder Creek to continue through lush forest to a spur (right) to Thunder Creek Camp near the creek about 2 miles from the campground.

Technically, there's no "rain forest" here, yet the green abundance of trees and plants gives the forest a richness that deserves the name. Great trees, vine maples arched with moss, moss-cushioned logs, flowers in every season. Don't hurry. Look carefully and truly see.

83. ROSS DAM

Features	▪	small waterfalls, great boulders, huge power dam
One way	▪	less than a mile
Elevation change	▪	500 feet down, 500 feet back up
Difficulty	▪	moderate to steep
Open	▪	spring to fall
Map	▪	Green Trails 48

There's more here than a hydroelectric power dam and a backwater lake that stretches north into Canada: a contrasting mixture, too, of Nature's tranquility and violence.

From I-5 north of Mount Vernon, turn east at Exit 230 onto North Cascades Highway 20 and continue to Marblemount. Drive north 24 miles to Colonial Creek Campground on Thunder Arm in North Cascades National Park.

Find the trailhead about 4 miles beyond the campground off a parking area on the left (north) side of the highway at 2,800 feet.

The path, off the left side of the parking area, drops down to a wooden bridge over cascading Happy Creek and a resting place between two small tumbling waterfalls. A tranquil destination on its own. (In another 50 yards or so, the trail affords a better view back at this small gorge and waterfall.)

Farther down, the path passes a huge slab of rock that toppled off some higher cliff and jammed itself into the gorge. As you pass this

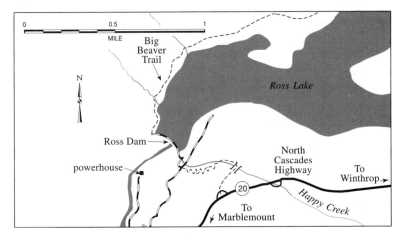

now-passive sign of violence, watch for a waypath to the left with a glimpse of still another waterfall.

Shortly, the trail starts a series of switchbacks down to a building perched on a bluff and the first full view down on the dam and out at the mountains. (Note here how a trail below follows the lakeshore to the right from the far side of the dam toward Beaver Creek and beyond.)

Still more switchbacks now lead down to a road to the right that goes to the top of the dam and to the left, dropping sharply to the powerhouse on Diablo Lake and the beginning of a trail there that winds west to the top of Diablo Dam. And, yes, of course, you can also walk across the dam and look down on its honeycombed concrete face. Yes, a dam's just a dam. But as the Northwest fills up with people, dams also sometimes become a very critical and important source of Seattle's light and heat.

Also bear in mind—hikers that hike down must also hike back up.

Ross Dam

84. CANYON CREEK

Features	■	forest, streams, history
One way	■	less than 1 mile
Elevation gain	■	none
Difficulty	■	easy
Open	■	summer
Map	■	Green Trails 49

Two creeks, two bridges, through lovely open forest to a place where two men, without roads or trails or bridges, decided to build a "home" ninety years ago.

From I-5 north of Mount Vernon, turn east at Exit 230 onto North Cascades Highway 20 and continue to Marblemount. Drive 32.8 miles to a trailhead off a parking area on Canyon Creek just below the highway on the left. From the east, drive west from Winthrop 55.1 miles.

The trail drops off the upriver end of the parking lot into a lovely forest bench, curving right to a bridge supported on sacks filled with concrete over Granite Creek.

Follow the low, level path down the creek to a house and then across a bridge over Canyon Creek. The trail to the left leads to a Forest Service barn that once housed mules and horses used to patrol this pristine area before the highway was built.

According to historians, the first cabin at the pleasant junction of these two creeks was built in 1902 by two sailors looking for gold. Twenty years later another prospector moved the house, one log at a

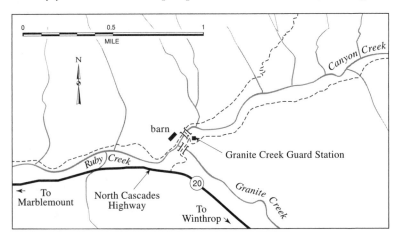

time, to where it now stands. It was used after that for more than twenty years as a Forest Service backcountry guard station.

This is a beautiful area. And it's plain why it served so long as someone's home. So treat all you find here with respect and care. Why destroy what was so difficult to build? Why desecrate such a pleasant place?

As someone else said: Have a little respect for history. And for the beauty that drew men here, even in a search for gold.

Historic cabin along Canyon Creek

85. RAINY LAKE

Features	■	classic high-mountain lake
One way	■	1 mile
Elevation gain	■	very slight
Difficulty	■	easy (for wheelchairs)
Open	■	summer
Map	■	Green Trails 50

A perfect mountain lake at 4,800 feet—with waterfalls from a glacier even—at the end of a paved mile-long trail through lovely subalpine forest.

From I-5 north of Mount Vernon, turn east at Exit 230 onto North Cascades Highway 20 and continue to Marblemount. Drive another 51 miles to Rainy Pass and a signed parking and picnic area south (to the right) of the highway.

Find the paved trail off the entrance (east) end of the parking loop.

This path, paved as it is, is part of the Engelmann spruce and Douglas fir forest here, hugging the natural contours of the slopes without any great engineering cuts or fills. With flower surprises. everywhere: monkey flowers soaking their roots in wet spots here and there, and paintbrush, spring beauties, and foam flowers everywhere.

Even highway noises that reach the trail are drowned out by occasional small, tumbling streams. Cool breezes brush the trail as you approach the lake, and downhill through the trees you can see a

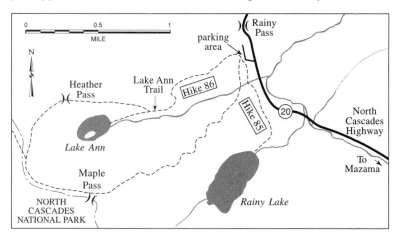

Rainy Lake

portion of the Pacific Crest Trail as it makes its way east and then south to Lake Chelan.

At Rainy Lake, find a viewing platform with benches and, more importantly, a vista filled with not-so-distant mountain ledges, terraces, snow, rock, and waterfalls below Lyall Glacier, itself tucked into the side of Frisco Mountain.

Don't, however, expect to enjoy this scenery alone. Visitors of every shape and form, in street shoes, sandals, even barefoot, in shorts, dresses, even bathing suits, walk this mile—as well they should—to see and take pictures of this rare scene. About halfway back to your car, note a trail on your left that zigzags steeply 1,800 feet up a ridge between Rainy Lake and Lake Ann (see Hike 86) and then loops down past Lake Ann in about 7.5 miles. Most hikers start the loop hike from the Lake Ann Trail.

191

86. LAKE ANN

Features	■	forests, lake, meadows
One way	■	2 miles
Elevation gain	■	700 feet
Difficulty	■	moderate to steep
Open	■	midsummer
Maps	■	Green Trails 49, 50

A pretty alpine lake with its own island and downstream ponds. And beyond, if you have the time and energy, higher alpine heather ridges with marmots, flowers, and still more vistas.

From I-5 north of Mount Vernon, turn east at Exit 230 onto North Cascades Highway 20 and continue to Marblemount. Drive another 51 miles to Rainy Pass and a signed parking and picnic area south (to the right) of the highway. (See map on page 190.)

Find the trail uphill to the right, off the entrance (east) end of the parking loop. It's signed.

The path to Lake Ann and beyond climbs easily the first 1.5 miles to a junction: Lake Ann to the left, Heather and Maple Passes to the right.

The Lake Ann Trail wends 0.5 mile around ponds and marshes, all worth strolling along, to the lake at 5,475 feet in a snow-fringed cirque with better views still. Marsh-loving flowers everywhere.

Lake Ann

The trail branch to Heather and Maple Passes climbs to views down on the lake before switchbacking to Heather Pass, a meadow-covered place at about 6,200 feet with limited vistas to the north.

After a traverse to the south, the trail then climbs to Maple Pass (6,600 feet) at the end of 3-plus miles, with still more meadows, marmots, and the most spectacular scenery of all. On clear weekends, watch for climbers on surrounding peaks nearby. You'll often hear them talking before you see them in the rocks. The path from Maple Pass that leads to Frisco Mountain joins a steep trail that drops down a ridge between Lake Ann and Rainy Lake and ends on the lower trail to Rainy Lake, a 0.5 mile from the beginning of the loop. Seven-plus miles around the entire loop.

87. BLUE LAKE

Features	■	high lake, meadows, peaks
One way	■	2.25 miles
Elevation gain	■	about 1,100 feet
Difficulty	■	moderate
Open	■	midsummer
Map	■	Green Trails 50

Look up at the cliffs of Liberty Bell and Early Winters Spires and north at Cutthroat Peak from the shores of a rock-rimmed mountain lake.

From I-5 north of Mount Vernon, turn east at Exit 230 onto North

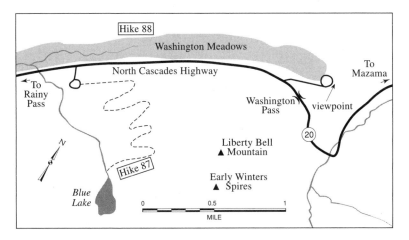

Blue Lake

Cascades Highway 20 and continue to Marblemount. Drive another 55 miles to a trailhead about 3 miles beyond Rainy Pass.

Find the trail off a parking area at the end of a short spur road to the right (south) of the highway.

The trail makes its way upward parallel to the highway for a long 0.25 mile before switchbacking away from the noisy road.

At the end of a long mile, the path climbs into an avalanche meadow with views, and in another 0.5 mile crosses a steep flower-covered meadow with still greater views below the towering crags of Liberty Bell. Note a mountain climbers' path to the left.

The trail reaches the outlet of the lake at 6,300 feet. A rock outcrop provides a picnic, resting, and viewing spot near an abandoned shelter. There's no formal trail around the lake. Take time, however, to explore the ridge to the right of the lake, with its pretty ponds and larches that glow golden in the fall.

No highway noises here, but on weekends listen for the calls of climbers on Liberty Bell and Early Winters Spires.

88. WASHINGTON MEADOWS

Features	▪	high, lush meadows, and Liberty Bell Mountain
One way	▪	set your own limit
Elevation gain	▪	none
Difficulty	▪	soggy
Open	▪	midsummer
Map	▪	Green Trails 50

The flowers and scenery here belong to the meadow at 5,500 feet. But the discoveries belong to you.

From I-5 north of Mount Vernon, turn east at Exit 230 onto North Cascades Highway 20 and continue to Marblemount and then on to Washington Pass. (See map on page 193.)

Find this meadow on the west (left) side of the entry road to Washington Pass Overlook. Park on the west side of the road (after you've visited the overlook, of course) and pick your own short path to the meadow.

You'll find no formal trails, although the Pacific Crest Trail crossed the meadows before the highway was constructed.

Unmarked paths below the road that start and then stop lead to meadow corners you'll be unable to resist, with views up at Liberty Bell—the peak that commands this place—that change with each new little creek, pond, and tree.

Two suggestions, though, before you start. First, be prepared for mosquitoes, tons of them, unless it's a breezy day. And second, this is a soggy place. In late fall you may be able to wander without getting your feet wet, but most of the time some sort of waterproof or rubber shoes will help.

Sometime-paths on the south and east sides of the meadow below the highway and entrance road are most likely to remain above the marshy waterline. Watch for deer tracks here and perhaps even bear tracks. And in the small ponds, frogs for sure, and in the streams, if you're lucky, the flash of a fleeing trout.

But it is the flowers that command the most attention in these meadows. Nature changes her bouquets here almost every week.

It would be pointless to try listing all the flowers. Cotton grass for sure. Gentians in the fall. Bog orchids and elephant's head without fail. You'll need a flower book.

Liberty Bell from Washington Meadows

Take nothing and destroy nothing as you walk here. Look only, so others can enjoy. Tenderness is the rule, and fragile is the reason why. And as you leave? Bow deeply to the mountain and applaud.

89. CUTTHROAT LAKE

Features ▪	alpine lake
One way ▪	2 miles
Elevation gain ▪	450 feet
Difficulty ▪	moderate
Open ▪	midsummer
Map ▪	Green Trails 50

As cars parked at the trailhead often indicate, this is a popular place. But take heart, many hikers use this as a jumping-off place for treks beyond the lake into the North Cascades.

Frolicking in Cutthroat Lake

From I-5 north of Mount Vernon, drive east on North Cascades Highway 20, finding the trailhead at the end of uphill Spur Road 400, about 4.6 miles beyond Washington Pass. Or from Winthrop, drive about 1.5 miles beyond Lone Fir Campground. (Even the view from Forest Road 400 is worth the trip.)

The trail starts in a heavily used sandy flat and then climbs gradually away from the creek to a junction in 1.75 miles. (The uphill trail to the right climbs sharply here to Cutthroat Pass in almost 4 miles. A shorter trip offers views down on the lake.)

The path left drops to the lake tucked into a circle of mountains at 4,935 feet in a short 0.25 mile. Picnic spots, flowers in their season, and endless views.

No camping within 200 feet of the lake.

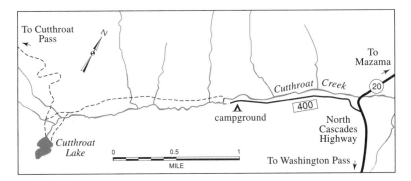

90. CEDAR FALLS

Features ■	waterfalls
One way ■	1.75 miles
Elevation gain ■	slight
Difficulty ■	easy, but slick rocks at falls
Open ■	spring
Map ■	Green Trails 51

Walk above noisy Cedar Creek to a tumble of waterfalls with resting places and views from slabs of rocks above the falls. A must for any falls collector.

From the west, drive east on North Cascades Highway 20 over Washington Pass to Klipchuck Campground, about 70 miles past Marblemount. From the east, drive 18 miles west of Winthrop.

About 0.3 mile beyond the campground, turn right (east) on Spur Road 200 (the road is signed "Trailhead" on the highway). Drive about 0.9 mile to a gravel pit, and find the trail uphill off the creek side of the pit.

The path climbs gradually above Cedar Creek through an open sidehill forest of fir and spruce with occasional stands of cedar.

You'll hear the waterfalls before you see them. Water here tumbles 50 feet or more in a series of falls from several crystal pools.

Warning: Wet rocks can be slippery here, and there are no fences or barriers. So pick your way with care on all of the steep sidehills and slopes around and above the falls. Not for uncontrolled children.

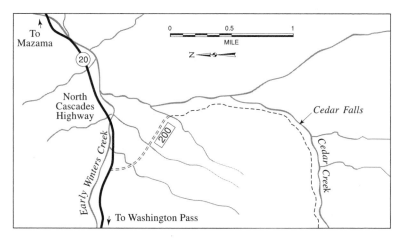

Cedar Falls

92. Slate Peak and High Meadows
PASAYTEN WILDERNESS
Harts Pass CG
Meadows CG
OKANOGAN NATIONAL FOREST
Tiffany Spring CG
97. Tiffany Lake
5400
Ballard CG
200
95. Falls Creek Falls
Chewuch River
93. Tatie Peak Ridge
5225
51
96. Freezeout Ridge
Methow River
River Bend CG
91. Goat Peak Lookout
Flat CG
37
37
Klipchuck CG
5130
Falls Creek CG
52
Early Winters CG
Mazama
20
Washington Pass
94. Sullivan's Pond
OKANOGAN NATIONAL FOREST
20
N
NORTH CASCADES NATIONAL PARK
Winthrop
Methow
Pearrygin Lake State Park CG
0   5   10
MILES
20
44
Black Pine – Twisp River Rd
River
Twisp
20
LAKE CHELAN NATIONAL RECREATION AREA
43
Black Pine Lake CG
200
153
98. Lookout Mountain

Eight Hikes Near Harts Pass and Twisp
Forest Road 5400/North Cascades Hwy 20

From the Pacific Crest Trail near Tatie Peak

EIGHT
HIKES NEAR
HARTS PASS
AND TWISP

FOREST ROAD 5400/NORTH CASCADES HIGHWAY 20

Two lookouts, the highest road in the state, an entrancing high-ridge trail, plus a waterfall.

Slate Peak (Hike 92) a former radar station site is the highest road in the state. **Lookout Mountain** (Hike 98) and **Goat Peak Lookout** (Hike 91) offer different mountain panoramas. **Sullivan's Pond** (Hike 94) provides the nesting birds and the **Tatie Peak Ridge Trail** (Hike 93) is beautifully and precisely that. **Falls Creek Falls** (Hike 95) is really two, one atop the other with a steep trail in-between.

For information on campgrounds nearby, see Appendix 1, Campgrounds. For current reports on trail and road conditions contact the Methow Valley Ranger Station or see the Okanogan–Wenatchee Forest Service website (see Appendix 2).

91. GOAT PEAK LOOKOUT

Features	■	vistas, vistas, vistas
One way	■	2.5 miles
Elevation gain	■	1,400 feet
Difficulty	■	moderate to steep
Open	■	midsummer
Map	■	Green Trails 51

Walk to absolutely the most stunning views in this entire area. From a lookout atop Goat Peak at 7,000 feet that you can see from practically every highway in the valley.

From I-5 north of Mount Vernon, drive east on North Cascades Highway 20 over Rainy and Washington Passes into the Methow Valley. Turn north (left) off the highway to Mazama, less than 2 miles east of the Early Winters Information Center.

Turn right at Mazama onto Mazama/Harts Pass/Lost River Road (depending on the map you use) and in about 2 miles turn sharply left uphill onto Forest Road 52. (From the east, drive west from Winthrop on Highway 20 and turn right in about 8 miles, just before the highway crosses the Methow River. Turn right again in 3.4 miles onto Forest Road 52.)

In 2.2 miles (on Forest Road 52), turn left onto Forest Road 5225. In 3.3 miles (great scenery here), turn right onto Spur Road 200, reaching the trailhead on the right in another 2.5 miles.

The trail starts out on a ridge, climbing alternately through meadows

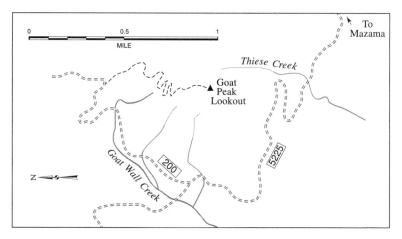

and open forest. In about 1 mile it settles down to the serious work of gaining elevation, topping out on the ridge to wander up and down through grand views and wildflowers to the lookout perched on the valley rim.

And from the lookout? Peaks everywhere. To the south, all of the Methow Valley and the North Cascades Highway, Silver Star Mountain with its glaciers, and Gardner Mountain to its left, plus, to the east, peaks of the Cascade Crest and, to the north and west, mountains within the Pasayten Wilderness.

Goat Peak Lookout

92. SLATE PEAK AND HIGH MEADOWS

Features	■	alpine meadows and views plus views
One way	■	2 miles or more
Elevation gain	■	200 feet
Difficulty	■	easy
Open	■	midsummer
Maps	■	Green Trails 18, 50

Two choices here. Pick them both.

The first leads through high meadows on the Pacific Crest Trail. The other to sweeping panoramas from the top of Slate Peak at 7,440 feet.

From I-5 north of Mount Vernon, drive east on North Cascades Highway 20 over Rainy and Washington Passes into the Methow Valley. Turn north (left) off the highway to Mazama, less than 2 miles east of the Early Winters Information Center.

Turn left in Mazama and follow the narrow and steep Harts Pass Forest Road 5400 for 18.5 miles to Harts Pass. At the pass turn north on Spur Road 600.

To hike through the high meadows along the Pacific Crest Trail, find the trailhead to the left at 6,000 feet off a hairpin turn in Spur Road 600 in about 1.5 miles.

The path drops gently downhill below Slate Peak and in less than 2 miles brings views of the old mining complex in Barron. All the buildings you see in the basin below the trail are on private mining

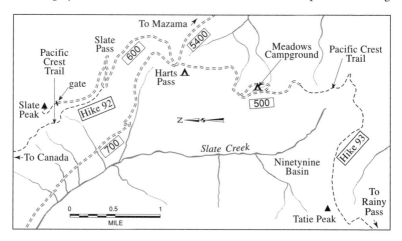

Hiking road to Slate Peak

claims, many of which have not been worked for decades. Note how slowly the mining wounds on the meadows have healed.

It's the steep meadows along the trail, however, with flowers, flowers, and flowers, that truly make any walk here for any distance worth every step and moment.

To reach the top of Slate Peak, the highest point (7,440 feet) in the state reached by a road, drive beyond the switchback on Spur Road 600 (see above) to a gate below a formal viewpoint. The mountain was flattened by the army for a radar station after World War II.

A 360-degree view here of the Cascade Crest. Displays identify surrounding peaks.

93. TATIE PEAK RIDGE

Features ■	high vistas and meadows
One way ■	2 miles or more
Elevation gain ■	600 feet
Difficulty ■	easy to steep
Open ■	midsummer
Maps ■	Green Trails 50; Okanogan–Wenatchee National Forest map

Follow the Pacific Crest Trail for a spectacular mile or two to sweeping views over open alpine meadows.

From I-5 north of Mount Vernon, drive east on North Cascades

Raccoon

Highway 20 over Rainy and Washington Passes into the Methow Valley and turn north (left) off the highway to Mazama, less than 2 miles east of the Early Winters Information Center.

Turn left in Mazama and follow the narrow and steep Harts Pass Road 5400 for 18.5 miles to Harts Pass. At the pass turn south on Spur Road 500 and follow it to the end beyond Meadows Campground. (See map on page 204.)

At the trailhead take the Pacific Crest Trail to the left as it climbs around the edge of a ridge above a once-upon-a-time private mining site and then turns north (still climbing) to a narrow ridge extending to Tatie Peak.

Truly breathtaking views from the ridge at 7,000 feet over Ninetynine Basin to the north and over the south fork of Trout Creek to the south. And in both directions: far, far beyond. Use an Okanogan–Wenatchee National Forest map to identify the surrounding peaks.

Pause here, certainly, and if you have the time, walk toward Tatie Peak. Just for the pleasure of it.

94. SULLIVAN'S POND

Features	■	pond and birds
One way	■	0.5-mile at most
Elevation gain	■	none
Difficulty	■	easy (no formal trails)
Open	■	spring to fall
Maps	■	Green Trails 52, 84

A wander here around a small but busy, bird-filled marshy pond. At its noisy best in the spring.

From I-5 north of Mount Vernon, turn east at Exit 230 onto North Cascades Highway 20 and continue to Winthrop, following signs from there north to Pearrygin Lake State Park at the eastern end of Pearrygin Lake. From the park entrance road, drive north about 0.2 mile. Turn left at a Y and find the unsigned pond on the left in less than 2 miles as the road suddenly climbs out of the dry, open slopes and enters forest.

(On the way up, enjoy the sweeping pictures back over Pearrygin Lake and out over Chewuch Valley ranches to the west from the road. Watch, too, for northern harriers, red-tailed hawks, and, with luck, a golden eagle.)

At the pond, find an unmarked parking area on the left, another one below the road midpond, and a third at the far end of the pond in a camplike parking spot below the road as it leaves the pond. All in the Methow Wildlife Refuge.

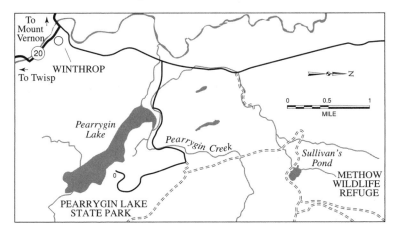

Sullivan's Pond

The best walking area is on the far side of the pond, off the camp-like parking area along an old road through open forest near the pond. Three-strand fences mark cattle grazing allotment boundaries here. Otherwise, pick a waiting spot—and wait.

But no matter where you stop, be patient. This small pond is a world of birds and animals that will show themselves only when they are ready. In the spring, red-wing and yellow-headed blackbirds, ducks of several sorts, coots, warblers, and, in the open forest around the pond, woodpeckers, ruffed grouse, nighthawks, and swallows, just to begin a list. And with the best of luck, deer grazing in the trees and muskrats and beavers in the pond.

95. FALLS CREEK FALLS

Features	▪ waterfalls
One way	▪ less than 0.5 mile
Elevation gain	▪ 75 feet
Difficulty	▪ moderate to steep
Open	▪ spring to fall
Map	▪ Green Trails 52

A short walk leads to a couple of frothy, talkative, pretty waterfalls with rock ledges for viewing.

Falls Creek falls

From I-5 north of Mount Vernon, turn east at Exit 230 onto North Cascades Highway 20 and continue to Winthrop, 89 miles past Marblemount.

From Winthrop, drive north on East Chewuch River Road (follow Pearrygin Lake signs out of town) along the east side of the Chewuch River. Turn left in about 6 miles and cross the river to paved Forest Road 51. Falls Creek and Falls Creek Campground are to the right in about 5.5 miles.

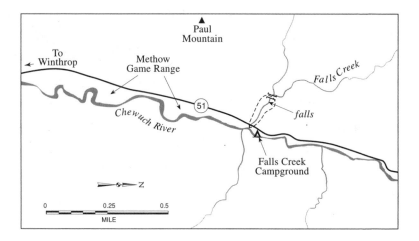

Find the waterfalls off a path that starts across the road from the campground, north of Falls Creek. The path continues uphill, to the right, beyond the first torrent to the second falls and then uphill on a steep scrabble trail to a viewpoint over the valley from a rock ledge.

Cross a bridge when you return to walk the path on the south side of the creek.

Pretty, even in the fall. Violent in the spring.

96. FREEZEOUT RIDGE

Features ▪	high meadow and distant views
One way ▪	2 miles or more
Elevation gain ▪	800 feet or more
Difficulty ▪	steep to very steep
Open ▪	summer
Map ▪	Green Trails 53

Hike about a mile (the elevation here at near 7,000 feet will make it seem much longer) to open meadows below Tiffany Mountain, once a lookout site at 8,242 feet.

From I-5 north of Mount Vernon, turn east at Exit 230 onto North Cascades Highway 20 and continue to Winthrop, 89 miles past Marblemount.

From Winthrop, drive north on East Chewuch River Road (follow Pearrygin Lake signs out of town) along the east side of the Chewuch River. Bear right in about 8 miles onto Forest Road 37.

Tiffany Mountain

In another 13 miles, bear left onto Forest Road 39 (Forest Road 37 continues east to Conconully), reaching Freezeout Pass and the trailhead at 6,500 feet in about 4 more miles.

(If you can spare a moment, stop en route at the primitive campground on Roger Lake, less than a mile from the pass, to observe the work of beavers. Note the trees standing in water now. Observe fresh repairs on small dams on creeks near the campground. And notice the overgrown ridges of dams built long ago. Beaver are credited with expanding the lake to the present size that you can observe from Freezeout Trail.)

At Freezeout Pass, find the ridge trail uphill to the right as it

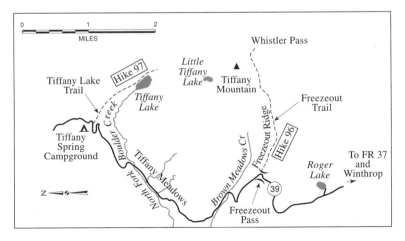

climbs steeply through toppled snags up what was once a road of some sort. Look down on Roger Lake from a spur path leading right in a saddle in about 0.75 mile.

The path reaches the low end of the meadow system, dotted with clusters of alpine fir, in about a mile. The flowers here at 7,000 feet barely peek above the grass.

Cairns mark unrutted sections of the path as it makes its way toward Tiffany Mountain. If you want, continue on a trail up to Whistler Pass around the right side of the mountain, or pick your way slowly up the open slopes to the summit. Or find a slab of rock and enjoy the meadow with its flowers, hawks, golden eagles (if you're lucky), deer, and views of the Cascade peaks—from 7,000 feet.

97. TIFFANY LAKE

Features	■ lake and meadows
One way	■ less than 2 miles
Elevation gain	■ 100 feet
Difficulty	■ easy
Open	■ summer
Map	■ Green Trails 53

An easy downhill walk on a sometimes soggy trail leads to a pretty lake with views of Tiffany Mountain.

From I-5 north of Mount Vernon, turn east at Exit 230 onto North Cascades Highway 20 and continue to Winthrop, 89 miles past Marblemount.

From Winthrop, drive north on East Chewuch River Road (follow Pearrygin Lake signs out of town) along the east side of the Chewuch River. In about 8 miles bear right onto Forest Road 37.

In another 13 miles bear left onto Forest Road 39 (Forest Road 37 continues east to Conconully), crossing Freezeout Pass in 4 miles and reaching Tiffany Spring Campground in another 4 miles. (See map on page 211.)

Find the trailhead across the road from the campground. The path leads gradually downhill to the lake in about a mile and then along the lake and through a soggy marsh. Fishing here, for sure. Marsh flowers when in season, too. And constant views up at Tiffany Mountain.

Tiffany Lake

At the end of the marshy area, the trail climbs steeply around the backside of the mountain to Tiffany Pass and then drops back to Freezeout Pass. A stiff and sometimes precarious 6.5-mile trip.

98. LOOKOUT MOUNTAIN

Features ▪	grand vistas from 5,518 feet
One way ▪	1.5 miles
Elevation gain ▪	1,200 feet
Difficulty ▪	steep
Open ▪	summer
Map ▪	Green Trails 54

A lookout, naturally, on a mountain of the same name. With sweeping panoramas over Twisp, the Methow Valley, the Columbia Basin, and all the surrounding ridges and peaks.

Lookout on Lookout Mountain

From I-5 north of Mount Vernon, turn east at Exit 230 onto North Cascades Highway 20 and continue to Marblemount, then 105 miles more over Washington Pass to Twisp.

In Twisp, drive west on the Black Pine–Twisp River Road, turning uphill to the left in about 0.2 mile onto paved Road Forest 200, signed "Lookout Mountain Trail." Limited views of the valley on the way to the trailhead at the end of the road in about 8 miles.

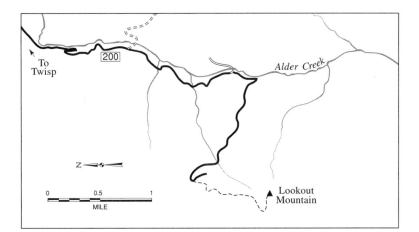

The trail makes its way uphill for less than 1.5 miles, ultimately topping out on a ridge and climbing sharply to the left another 0.25 mile to the lookout, staffed sometimes in the summer. And don't ask, as some do, for a drink of water. Just remember, those in the lookout tower have to carry their water, too.

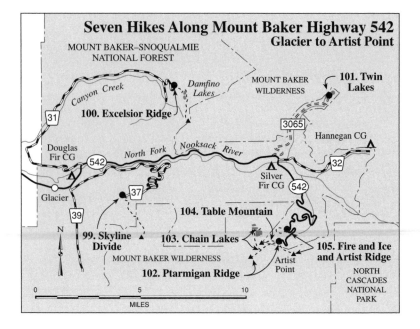

Seven Hikes Along Mount Baker Highway 542
Glacier to Artist Point

MOUNT BAKER–SNOQUALMIE
NATIONAL FOREST

Canyon Creek

Damfino Lakes

MOUNT BAKER
WILDERNESS

101. Twin Lakes

31

100. Excelsior Ridge

3065

Hannegan CG

Douglas
Fir CG

542

North Fork *Nooksack River*

32

37

Silver
Fir CG

542

Glacier

39

N

104. Table Mountain

99. Skyline Divide

103. Chain Lakes

MOUNT BAKER WILDERNESS

102. Ptarmigan Ridge

Artist
Point

105. Fire and Ice and Artist Ridge

NORTH
CASCADES
NATIONAL
PARK

0   5   10

MILES

Mount Baker from Artist Point

SEVEN
HIKES ALONG
MOUNT BAKER
HIGHWAY 542

GLACIER TO ARTIST POINT

Meet Mount Baker face to face. What's more to say? Bring a sack of adjectives and wish that you'd brought more!

Start with **Skyline Divide** (Hike 99). The mountain fills the skyline to the south. Even from **Twin Lakes** (Hike 101), at the end of an uncertain road, Winchester Mountain Lookout amplifies the volcano once again. From **Ptarmigan Ridge** (Hike 102) Mount Baker still, but with ridges filled with alpine huckleberries in the fall. And finally, **Table Mountain** (Hike 104). Make a short steep climb, pick a restful slab of rock and then fill your sack of adjectives again. For the poem that you'll write, of course.

For information on campgrounds nearby, see Appendix 1, Campgrounds. To update reports on trail and road conditions contact the Mount Baker Ranger Station, Glacier Public Service Center, and see the Mount Baker–Snoqualmie National Forest website (see Appendix 2).

99. SKYLINE DIVIDE

Features	■	meadows and Mount Baker
One way	■	2 miles
Elevation gain	■	1,400 feet
Difficulty	■	steep
Open	■	summer
Map	■	Green Trails 13

A 2-mile hike up a forested trail brings its final reward: a tremendous panorama of Mount Baker, Mount Shuksan, and Excelsior Ridge from a flower-in-season alpine ridge at about 5,900 feet.

Turn east off I-5 at Exit 255 in Bellingham onto Mount Baker Highway 542 and drive about 0.5 mile east of the Glacier Public Service Center. Turn south (right) on Glacier Creek Forest Road 39. Then, in about 300 feet, turn east (left) on Deadhorse Forest Road 37, driving about 12 miles to the trailhead parking area. Views here over the Nooksack Valley toward Excelsior Ridge and Church and Bearpaw Peaks.

The trail climbs sharply through the forest with the first views in about a mile and the first meadows in 2 miles at about 5,800 feet. You'll be tempted to continue toward the mountain and the end of the trail in another 1.5 miles. But the flower meadows (in early summer) or huckleberry meadows (in the fall) and all of their accompanying glory remain pretty much the same now no matter how far you go—with Mount Baker all the time. Grand. Grander. Grandest.

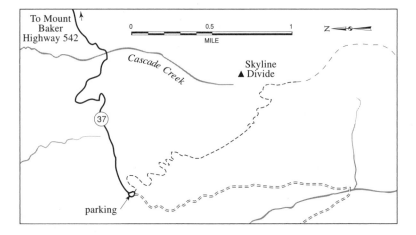

Mount Baker from Skyline Divide

So take time for lunch, to read, to nap. To enjoy the pleasures of a flower, observe the marmot's den, watch fairy figures in the clouds. Or just wander aimlessly.

And there's space for everyone. You can't get lost—except in your deepest private thoughts.

100. EXCELSIOR RIDGE

Features	■	small lakes and big mountain scenery
One way	■	3 miles
Elevation gain	■	1,100 feet
Difficulty	■	moderate
Open	■	late spring to early fall
Map	■	Green Trails 13

Hike past two pretty tarnlike lakes, through forest, and across lush meadows to a high ridge that overlooks the best of everything.

From I-5 at Bellingham, turn east at Exit 255 to Mount Baker Highway 542 and head north about 2 miles east of the Glacier Public

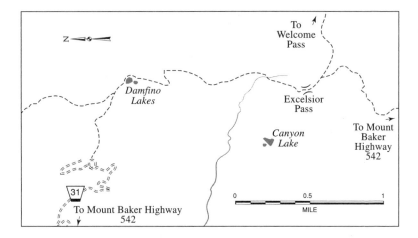

Service Center, just beyond the Douglas Fir Campground, onto Canyon Creek Forest Road 31. Drive to the marked and developed trailhead near the end of the road in about 15 miles.

(On Forest Road 31, search for leaf-imprinted rocks alongside the road just short of the 4-mile marker. Black crumbly rocks contain matted fossils of ancient stems and stalks.)

Mount Baker from Excelsior Pass

The trail to the ridge starts out in a clear-cut, quickly enters forest, and soon skirts the two small Damfino Lakes. Trail bikes are supposed to turn left here for other trails to the north. You turn right and follow a hiker trail uphill through more forest, crossing several meadows and dropping slightly before climbing to Excelsior Pass at 5,300 feet.

Explosive scenes here of Baker, Church, and Bearpaw Peaks and the endless clear-cut blotches in the forests of Canyon Creek basin.

Hike up the knoll to the east to a former lookout site at 5,700 feet, following the ridge trail east. Or simply wander the open meadows as you wish to find your own personal observation, rest, or luncheon spot.

From the pass, trails drop down the mountain to the highway (4.5 miles) or wander eastward along the ridge to Welcome Pass (4.5 miles) and, again, down to the highway.

101. TWIN LAKES

Features	■	lakes, meadows, vistas
One way	■	about 2.5 miles
Elevation gain	■	1,600 feet
Difficulty	■	moderate
Open	■	midsummer
Map	■	Green Trails 14

For many this hike is only a beginning, but as a short hike it's a worthy end itself.

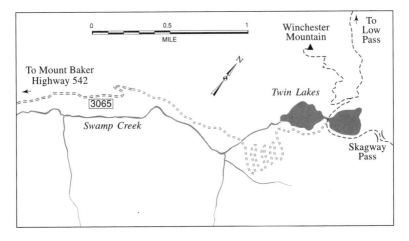

Mount Baker from Twin Lakes

The road here serves two masters. The first and longest section is a Forest Service road. The last section, very rough and sometimes chancy, is a mine-to-market road built to access a now inactive mine; it is seldom (if ever) maintained by the mine owner. However, the ugliness of the road disappears once you reach the plateau that cradles the twin crystal lakes.

From I-5 at Bellingham, turn east at Exit 255 to Mount Baker Highway 542. Turn north 13 miles east of the Glacier Public Service Center onto Forest Road 3065, just uphill beyond the highway maintenance barns at Shuksan. The forest service road ends in about 4.5 miles near the Tomyhoi Lake Trail. Some park there and walk the rest of the way. Many, however, take the chance and bounce through all the ruts.

But whatever your path, the scenes get better the farther you go. For once the "road" reaches the lakes at 5,200 feet: Heaven. Pure heaven. Crystal lakes amid heather meadows surrounded by mountain peaks.

All sorts of places for pleasant wandering and resting here. Paths this way and that. There's even a picnic table or two.

The trail, to High/Low Pass, climbs north between the lakes, ending in 4 miles at an abandoned mine. Within 0.25 mile, another trail climbs west 1.5 miles to a lookout atop Winchester Mountain, where panoramas end just short of heaven.

But it's not necessary to go the entire way on any trail here. A short walk beyond Low Pass leads across flower meadows to views of peaks beyond the Canadian border to the north. And although the lookout on Winchester Mountain is a worthy goal, a walk even part way offers views back down on Twin Lakes and more flower meadows, too. Other paths lead east to Skagway Pass and the mining sites for which the road was built.

One warning: Steep patches of summer snow can be dangerous on all these trails. Unless you are properly equipped, turn back.

102. PTARMIGAN RIDGE

Features	■	high meadows and mountain splendors
One way	■	2 miles
Elevation gain	■	400 feet in, 150 feet out
Difficulty	■	moderate
Open	■	midsummer
Map	■	Green Trails 14

You can't avoid the sense of mountains here. Steep flower meadows, rock-strewn slopes, huckleberries, marmots whistling everywhere. And snowcapped mountains no matter where you turn. Nature commands these slopes and meadows. Humans have a right to visit only as guests.

From I-5 in Bellingham, turn east at Exit 255 to Mount Baker Highway 542. Drive 67 miles to the end of the paved highway in a huge parking lot at Artist Point, on Kulshan Ridge at 5,100 feet, 2 miles beyond and above the Mount Baker ski complex.

The broad trail drops down from the end of the parking lot and

Mount Shuksan from Ptarmigan Ridge

proceeds the first easy mile into the Mount Baker Wilderness across a sloping meadow stuffed with flowers (find the shy magenta paintbrush here). Allow time to whistle with the marmots, tempt the chipmunks, and chatter with the pikas that scamper through the rocks.

At the trail junction (Hike 103, Chain Lakes to the right), continue straight ahead to crest the saddle and follow the trail downhill across scree and rocks toward Ptarmigan Ridge, noting as you go that even amid these tumbled broken stones small flowers grow.

In another mile, the trail climbs the ridge to camping and picnic spots on huckleberry and heather meadows. Plus vistas, yes, that never seem to end.

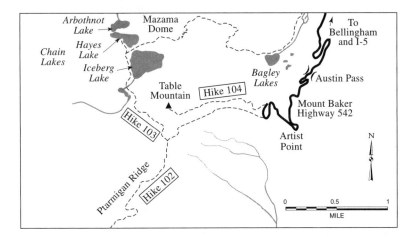

The way continues another 3.5 miles to an unmarked climbers' camp. (Snow sometimes covers the trail on this ridge all summer long, so judge your skills and equipment before you proceed.)

If you can, walk at least another mile. The changing spectacle will take your breath away. Mount Baker, Coleman Pinnacle, Mount Shuksan, with other distant mountains everywhere.

And all through dwarf huckleberry meadows in the fall, flowers in late spring and summer, snow patches year-round, and heather everywhere.

103. CHAIN LAKES

Features ■	lakes, meadows, mountains
One way ■	1.75 miles
Elevation change ■	drop 500 feet and climb 100 feet going in
Difficulty ■	steep in places
Open ■	midsummer
Map ■	Green Trails 14

A cluster of mountain lakes set in subalpine forests amid heather and huckleberry meadows—all part of, but away from, the dominating mountains in the Mount Baker Wilderness and nearby North Cascades National Park.

From I-5 in Bellingham, turn east at Exit 255 to Mount Baker Highway 542. Drive some 67 miles to the end of the paved highway in a huge parking lot at Artist Point, on Kulshan Ridge at 5,100 feet,

Mount Baker from Iceberg Lake

2 miles beyond and above the Mount Baker ski complex. (See map on page 225.)

The broad trail drops from the parking lot and proceeds the first easy mile toward the mountain across steep flower meadows filled with marmots, chipmunks, and pikas scampering in the rocks, with views of Mounts Baker and Shuksan from every point along the way.

At the trail junction at the end of the steeply sloping meadow, take the trail to the right over a 5,200-foot ridge to Chain Lakes. (The trail straight ahead goes to Ptarmigan Ridge, Hike 102.)

The trail drops 1 mile through several small meadows filled with tiny private streams before climbing slightly to Iceberg Lake at 4,500 feet. Some years you will find ice floating on Iceberg Lake all summer long.

Stop here or press on to Hayes and Arbothnot Lakes, only a short way farther on. To see Hayes Lake, either turn right on the trail that loops back to the ski area in 4.75 miles or walk straight ahead on a path that also proceeds on to Arbothnot Lake.

Prowl all the lakes and then return the way you came—unless you want to struggle steeply up and down to the highway at the ski area.

104. TABLE MOUNTAIN

Features	■	alpine gardens with vistas, vistas, vistas
One way	■	1 mile
Elevation gain	■	600 feet
Difficulty	■	steep all the way
Open	■	mid- to late summer
Map	■	Green Trails 14

You'll need persistence here for sure. There are few flat sections on this trail. And as you go up—there is no going down at all.

But every effort, every promise to yourself to never come this way again, will be forgotten in the end. For what you see and remember here will overwhelm every moment's pain.

From I-5 in Bellingham, turn east at Exit 255 to Mount Baker Highway 542. Drive some 67 miles to the end of the paved highway in a huge parking lot at Artist Point, on Kulshan Ridge at 5,100 feet, 2 miles beyond and above the Mount Baker ski complex. (See map on page 225.)

The trail starts behind a sign on the uphill side of the parking area and then switchbacks steadily and steeply to the top of the mountain.

Let all speedy hikers pass, remembering: The fabled turtle beat the rushing hare.

But even if the grade presents no pain, this is not a trail to hurry up but to stop on often to view the enormous scenes that spread out before you in ever-changing modes.

And take time, too, to explore short spur trails to other scenes and sometime-tarns and to enjoy the flowers in the summer and huckleberries in the fall (if you manage to get there before others have picked them all) before settling down to the switchbacks that climb up and across the rocky slope. You'll need to use your compound lower gear on stretches here for sure.

And take no shortcuts either going up or coming down. A loose rock can pose a danger not only to you but to those on the trail below you if it should fall.

At the top, veer to the left to wend your way less strenuously across the Table's top.

For most hikers, the top of the plateau at 5,700 feet will be the final goal. So once there, relax, wander, look around. Rest atop a boulder here, run your fingers through the mountain heather there. Find a huckleberry (if it's fall) in the little bushes at your feet. And wonder how a flower could possibly grow on that rock over there.

The trail continues across and down the backside of the mountain. But unless your mountain judgment is good, return the way you came. The far trail down the mountain is steep all the time, risky in spring, and unsafe always when snow is on the path.

And never forget your binoculars and camera, whether you plan to hike to the first ledge or the last. In addition to scenery: scurrying pikas, whistling marmots, and beautiful wildflowers at every turn.

Table Mountain and Mount Shuksan

105. FIRE AND ICE AND ARTIST RIDGE

Features	■	alpine environmental displays
One way	■	Fire and Ice, 0.5 mile; Artist Ridge, 1 mile
Elevation gain	■	modest
Difficulty	■	easy (wheelchair access)
Open	■	midsummer
Maps	■	Green Trails 14; Forest Service Heather Meadows map

Defined samples here of the best in alpine scenery, plants, animals, and geology. All from two easy loop trails near the end of Mount Baker Highway 542, but with enormous weekend crowds since the old rough gravel road was paved beyond the ski complex.

From I-5 in Bellingham, turn east at Exit 255 to Mount Baker Highway 542. Drive about 65 miles to the Mount Baker ski complex.

Fire and Ice Trail. Find the trail off a parking lot to the right (west) of the highway near Austin Pass (4,700 feet) beyond the visitor center and ski complex where the road starts its sharp uphill climb to Artist Point on Kulshan Ridge.

You'll find no views here of Mount Baker or Mount Shuksan to divert you. Here, tucked in a valley below Table Mountain and Mount Herman, you'll have time to study the flowers along the trails, to identify the pikas, ravens, hawks, and chipmunks living here, and to consider the geology that shaped the basin.

The path starts out across slopes of upended columnar basalt,

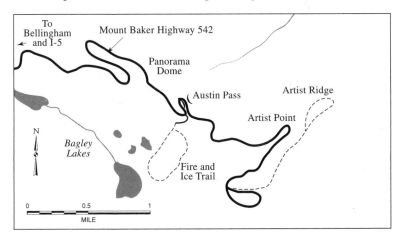

ground by glaciers into a classic honeycomb floor, and then wanders beside other bent and twisted columns stacked vertically like a fence.

Weathered and stunted mountain hemlock stand like strangers in the meadows here. Many of these stunted trees—thick at the bottom, small at the top, and not very tall because they've had so little time in the short alpine summers to add growth anywhere except near their roots—are more than 700 years old.

Follow the paved trail, designed for wheelchairs, downhill off the parking lot to displays overlooking Bagley Lakes. (A shorter paved loop at the beginning of the trail provides a less arduous wheelchair loop.)

From the lake overlook, a gravel trail leads to the left and circles gradually back up to the parking area along a little stream, through heather and huckleberry meadows filled with avalanche lilies in the early summer, and yellow alpine monkey flowers near small streams in the fall.

Unmarked trails lead down from the overlooks to the lake and other trails that cross the basin to Chain Lakes and the Austin Pass picnic area.

Formal displays explain most of the features along the way. And early in the summer, watch for skiers on the steep slopes to the west and south.

Artist Ridge Trail. Find the trail off the huge parking lot (5,100 feet) at the end of the highway. This hike offers a prime sample of a barren alpine terrain touched here and there with flowered and heathered patches of earth all guarded by alpine trees.

The trail starts to the right of the restroom at the entrance to the parking area. A paved path for wheelchairs leads to the first display. Gravel paths and rock steps lead around the rest of this truly alpine loop. Mount Shuksan and Mount Baker are constant companions here with mountains in Canada looking over ridges to the north.

Here, too, printed displays explain the geologic forces that shaped this rocky point and identify the plants, birds, and animals to be seen along the trail.

Near the end, the trail winds past little tarns and a point over-looking Swift Creek valley to a pond and a quotation from Aldo Leopold: "sit quietly and listen, think hard of everything you've seen, and try to understand."

Mount Baker from Artist Point

APPENDIX 1
CAMPGROUNDS

Most campgrounds listed here are closed during the winter, with opening and closing dates dependant on weather conditions. For current conditions and advance reservations opportunities, check with Forest Service ranger stations and headquarters of state and national parks (see Appendix 2). Single campsites in all campgrounds are available on a first-come, first-served basis. Campsites can be reserved in advance in many campgrounds. Fees vary from campground to campground and year to year.

INTERSTATE 90: NORTH BEND TO CLE ELUM

HIKES 1–5

Tinkham. 48 units in a forested campground on the south fork of the Snoqualmie River. Turn south off I-90 at Exit 42 (Tinkham Road); campground on the river side of the road. Toilets. Water. Fee. Group and individual reservations.

Denny Creek. 33 units in a series of loops. Some sites near the river, others in pleasant forest. Heavily used. Turn off I-90 at Exit 45 and loop over the freeway; campground in about 2.5 miles. Group and individual reservations. Toilets. Water. Fee. Reservations.

HIKES 6–12

Crystal Springs. 25 units between the Yakima River and I-90 off Exit 62. Sounds of the highway overpower sounds of the river. Pit toilets. Water. Fee.

Kachess. 150 units in a forested peninsula between Kachess and Little Kachess Lakes. 5 miles north of I-90 at Exit 62. Some sites near the lake, others near Gale Creek. Restrooms. Water. Fee. Group and individual reservations.

Wish Poosh. 39 units on forested loops on Cle Elum Lake. 8 miles from Cle Elum on Highway 903. Restrooms. Water. Swimming beach. Fee.

Cle Elum River. 35 units in pleasant, open forest near the Cle Elum River. 15 miles from Cle Elum on Highway 903. Toilets. Water. Fee.

Red Mountain. 12 units near the Cle Elum River. 16 miles north of Cle Elum on Highway 903. Toilets.

Owhi. 21 walk-in tent sites on Cooper Lake. 23 miles from Cle Elum (5 miles west of Highway 903). Toilets.

Salmon la Sac. 127 units on forested loops, some near the river. 25 miles from Cle Elum on Highway 903. Toilets. Water. Fee. Group and individual reservations.

Fish (Tucquala) Lake. 4 units near the Forest Service cabin 29 miles from Cle Elum on Forest Road 4330. Toilet. (Note: Sites in a once-upon-a-time campground on the river before you reach the ranger cabin are now occupied on a long-term basis by residents from nearby towns. You are entitled to wonder how and why.)

U.S. HIGHWAY 97: CLE ELUM TO CHELAN
HIKES 13–16

Beverly. 16 units in an open, wooded area along the north fork of the Teanaway River. Most sites oriented to the river. On Forest Road 9737 about 17 miles from U.S. 97, or 25 miles from Cle Elum. Toilets. Fee.

Mineral Springs. 12 sites at the junction of Medicine and Swauk Creeks. Just off U.S. 97, 3 miles north of the Liberty Guard Station, or 23 miles from Cle Elum. Group sites. Toilets. Water. Fee.

Swauk. 23 sites on wooded loops below U.S. 97 on Swauk Creek. Some sites near the creek, others in shady timber. Elevation 3,000 feet. Nature trail. Toilets. Fee.

HIKES 17–21

Entiat City Park. 81 units in an open area on Entiat Lake, behind Rocky Reach Dam on the Columbia River. Restrooms. Water. Fee. Reservations.

Pine Flat. 7 units on a flat on Mad River. Off Forest Road 5700, 5 miles northeast of Ardenvoir. Steep entrance road. Pit toilet.

Fox Creek. 15 units on a tree-shaded flat on the Entiat River. 27 miles east of Entiat. All units back from the river. Group sites. Toilets. Water. Fee.

Lake Creek. 18 units located on a bench above the river. 28 miles from Entiat. Pit toilets. Water. Fee.

Silver Falls. 35 sites on pleasant, forested loops on either side of Silver Creek. Some sites near the Entiat River. 30 miles from Entiat. Group sites. Toilets. Water. Fee.

North Fork. 9 units at the end of the paved road just beyond Entiat Falls. About 32 miles from Entiat. Pit toilets. Water. Fee.

Cottonwood. 27 sites at the end of Forest Road 51. 38 miles from Entiat. Pit toilets. Water. Fee.

Lake Chelan State Park. 201 sites along Lake Chelan. 9 miles west of Chelan. Popular area. Restrooms. Water. Fee. Group and individual reservations.

U.S. 2: GOLD BAR TO STEVENS PASS
HIKES 22–33

Wallace Falls State Park. 6 walk-in, tent-only units off a parking lot. No camping facilities for trailers or campers. Always full in summer. Restrooms. Water. Fee. Closed some days in the winter.

Troublesome Creek. 18 units on a forested loop. 11 miles north of U.S. 2 on Forest Road 63. Most sites near the river. Some equipped for wheelchair campers. Sites both east and west of the bridge. Popular on weekends. Nature trail. Pit toilets.

San Juan. 8 units near the north fork of the Skykomish River. About 1.25 miles beyond Troublesome Creek Campground (above). Pit toilets.

Money Creek. 24 units, some near the river, some on forested loops. A busy camp just off U.S. 2. 4 miles west of Skykomish. Toilets. Water. Fee.

Miller River. 100 group units by reservation only. Reservable as single sites, if available. 3 miles south of U.S. 2 on Forest Road 6412. Toilets. Water. $75.00 daily fee.

Beckler River. 27 units on a pleasant, forested loop near, but not on, the Beckler River. 1 mile north of Skykomish. Toilets. Water. Fee. Group and individual reservations.

U.S. 2: STEVENS PASS TO WENATCHEE
HIKES 34–39

Lake Wenatchee State Park. 197 units on both sides of the Wenatchee River outlet. Most sites away from the lake. An extremely heavily used area. Swimming. Boating. Restrooms. Water. Showers. Fee. Reservations.

Nason Creek. 76 units on both sides of Forest Road 6707 leading to the state park. Has been mistaken for the state park. Popular trailer area. Pit toilets. Water. Fee.

Glacier View. 23 sites in a very pleasant campground at the far end of South Shore Lake Wenatchee Road 6607. Walk-in tent sites from parking spurs on a campground loop. Some sites on the lake. Steep and narrow entrance road. No trailers. Pit toilets. Water. Fee.

Soda Springs. 5 sites in forest near the Wenatchee River. 8 miles west of Lake Wenatchee off Forest Road 65. Steep entrance road. No trailers. Soda spring. Pit toilets.

White River Falls. 5 units on the White River. 9 miles from Lake Wenatchee off Forest Road 6400. Waterfall attracts heavy vehicle traffic through the small camp. Steep and narrow entrance road. No trailers. Pit toilets. Water. Fee.

Tumwater. 84 units in a wooded area between Chiwaukum Creek and the Wenatchee River. 9 miles northwest of Leavenworth on U.S. 2. A popular, heavily used campground. Toilets. Water. Fee.

HIKES 40–43

Eightmile. 45 units on loops off Icicle Creek Road 76. About 8 miles from Leavenworth. Toilets. Water. Fee. Group and individual reservations.

Bridge Creek. 6 sites on Icicle Creek Road 76. 9 miles from Leavenworth. Pit toilets. Water. Fee.

Johnny Creek. 65 units on loops north and south of Icicle Creek Road 76. 12 miles from Leavenworth. Some near Icicle Creek. Most in pleasant forest settings. Toilets. Water. Fee.

Ida Creek. 10 units 14 miles up the Icicle River Road. Toilets. Water. Fee.

Chatter Creek. 12 units on forested loops above the road on two small forks of Chatter Creek. Off Icicle Creek Road 76 near the Chatter Creek Ranger Station. 17 miles from Leavenworth. Group sites. Pit toilets. Water. Fee.

Rock Island. 22 sites on wooded loops off Icicle Creek Road 76. 19 miles from Leavenworth. Some sites near the river. Often full. Pit toilets. Water. Fee.

Wenatchee River County Park. 100 sites in an open, grassy area with shade trees. On the Wenatchee River. Popular. 3-plus miles east of Cashmere on the south side of U.S. 2. Open all year. Restrooms. Water. Fee.

MOUNTAIN LOOP HIGHWAY: GRANITE FALLS TO DARRINGTON
HIKES 44–53

Turlow. 19 units in a wooded area across from the Verlot Information Station. Some sites near the river. Pit toilets. Water. Fee. Reservations.

Verlot. 25 units in a popular campground. 2.4 miles east of Verlot. Generally full most weekends but pleasantly private during the week. Restrooms. Water. Fee. Reservations.

Gold Basin. 92 units in another popular campground. Full most weekends. Some sites near the river but most on pleasant, forested loops. Restrooms. Water. Fee. Reservations.

Red Bridge. 16 units on a forested bend in the river. 7.1 miles east of Verlot. Heavy trailer use. Toilets. Water. Fee. Reservations.

Note: Several small camps without water and for groups by reservation can be found between Verlot and Barlow Pass.

HIKES 54–57

Bedal Creek. 18 units on a forested loop at the juncture of the Sauk and its north fork. Pit toilets. Fee. Reservations.

White Chuck. 5 units near the confluence of the White Chuck and Sauk Rivers. Just north of the White Chuck bridge. Pit toilets.

Clear Creek. 10 units between Mountain Loop Highway and the Sauk River. Only 9 miles from Darrington. Tends to get heavy local use. Pit toilets. Reservations.

Squire Creek. 34 well-developed units in old forest. 4 miles west of Darrington on Highway 530. Some sites near Squire Creek. A Snohomish County park. Restroom. Water. Fee.

ISLANDS IN THE PUGET SOUND

HIKES 58–59 (Moran State Park)

Warning: All camping in Moran State Park between May 15 and September 15 is limited to those with reservations made in advance through 880-CAMPOUT (226-7688). Campsites are available without reservations only between September 16 and May 14. The special May to September limitations are required due to heavy public demands, limited camping space, lack of private campgrounds on the island, and the limitations of ferry access. There is a $10 fee per night for a standard site and an $18 fee per night for a utility site, plus a one-time $7 service charge.

North End. 52 sites above the road on a shady slope just beyond the park entrance. Beach and recreation center on Cascade Lake just across the road. Restroom. Piped water.

Midway. 49 sites beyond the Cascade Lake Recreation Area. On wooded loops. Restrooms. Piped water.

South End. 17 sites, most near the water, at the south end of Cascade Lake. The oldest and most popular area in the park. Generally full. Restrooms. Piped water.

Mountain Lake. 18 sites near the lake on a peninsula beyond the landing/boat launch area at the end of the road to the lake. Restrooms. Piped water.

HIKES 60–64

San Juan County Park. 18 sites on an open bluff overlooking Haro Strait on the west side of San Juan Island. The only public campground on the island. From the Friday Harbor ferry terminal, drive west on Spring Street, bearing left on San Juan Valley Road, left again onto Douglas Road, and right on Bailer Hill Road. Continue generally westward on West Side Road, which overlooks the Strait, and turn inland at Lime Kiln Point, reaching the park above the Strait in a total of about 10 miles. Restrooms. Water. Fee.

HIKES 65–68 (Deception Pass State Park)

Bowman Bay. 16 sites on Bowman Bay north of Deception Pass. Sites on a wooded loop overlooking the bay. Often full. Summer only. Restrooms. Piped water. Fee. Reservations.

Forest Camp. 235 sites on forested loops north of Cranberry Lake. South of Deception Pass. Some sites open all year. Restroom. Piped water. Fee. Reservations.

Note: If you camp near Deception Pass, you may find the noise, particularly at night, unbearable. Jet fighters from the nearby naval air station sometimes sound like they may fly right through your tent.

HIKES 69–70

Washington Park (Anacortes). 75 sites, many with water and electrical hookups. All in a forested area. At the end of the road west of Anacortes beyond the ferry terminal. Restrooms. Fee.

NORTH CASCADES HIGHWAY 20: BAKER LAKE TO CASCADE PASS
HIKES 71–76

Kulshan. 40 sites west of Upper Baker Lake Dam. 13.3 miles from Highway 20 on Baker Lake Road and Forest Road 11. A Puget Power campground. Flush toilets. Piped water. No fee.

Horseshoe Cove. 34 units in timbered area near the lake. 14.8 miles from Highway 20 on Baker Lake Road and Forest Road 11. Swimming area; no lifeguard. Concessionaire-operated. Flush toilets. Piped water. Fee. Reservations.

Boulder Creek. 8 units in a wooded site along a glacial creek. 17.4 miles from Highway 20 on Baker Lake Road and Forest Road 11. Pit toilets. Group sites. Fee. Reservations.

Panorama Point. 16 units. 19.4 miles from Highway 20 on Baker Lake Road and Forest Road 11. Sites near water, but with little beach. Mountain views. Concessionaire-operated. Pit toilets. Water. Fee. Reservations.

Park Creek. 12 units on a creek off Forest Road 1144. Pit toilets. Fee. Reservations.

Shannon Creek. 20 units in a wooded area near the north end of the lake. 22.8 miles from Highway 20 on Baker Lake Road and Forest Road 11. Most sites on wooded loops away from the lake. Pit toilets. Fee. Reservations.

HIKES 77–78

Rockport State Park. 50 drive-in and walk-in tent sites on forested loops. 1 mile west of Rockport. Restrooms. Water. Nature trails. Fee. Reservations.

Steelhead Park Campground. 39 sites in an open area on the Skagit River. At Rockport. A Skagit county park. Open all year. Group sites. Restrooms. Water. Fee.

HIKES 79–80

Cascade Island. 15 sites along the Cascade River. A Department of Natural Resources campground on the south side of the river. About 2.5 miles from Marblemount. Early summer to fall. Pit toilets.

Marble Creek. 24 units, some along the river, others back on pleasant, forested loops. 9 miles from Marblemount. Narrow road may be difficult for trailers. Pit toilets. Fee. Reservations.

Mineral Park. 8 units in a pleasant, forested grove on the east side of the north fork of the Cascade River. Loops west of the river are closed. Pit toilets. Reservations.

Johannesburg Camp. Primitive hiker camp near the trailhead to Cascade Pass at the end of the road from Marblemount. Pit toilet.

NORTH CASCADES HIGHWAY 20: NEWHALEM TO EARLY WINTERS
HIKES 81–88

Goodell Creek. 21 units in a wooded area along the Skagit River. Open all year. Water. Toilets. Fee in summer.

Newhalem Creek. 129 units on forested loops south of the highway and across the Skagit River. Closed in winter. Nature trails. Naturalist programs. Restrooms. Water. Fee. Group and individual reservations.

Colonial Creek. 162 units on wooded loops, some near the shore of Thunder Arm on Diablo Lake. Closed in winter. Nearby trails. Naturalist programs. Restrooms. Water. Fee. Group and individual reservations.

HIKES 89–90

Lone Fir. 27 units on a loop near Early Winters Creek. 5 miles east of Washington Pass at 3,600 feet. Views of nearby peaks. Toilets. Water. Fee.

Klipchuck. 46 units in pleasant, open pine forest. Sites above Early Winters Creek. 3 miles west of the Early Winters Information Center.

HARTS PASS TO TWISP
FOREST ROAD 5400/NORTH CASCADES HIGHWAY 20
HIKES 91–93

Note: Trailers are prohibited on Harts Pass Road. Trailer camping can be found at Early Winters Campground.

Early Winters. 13 units in dry, open forest at 2,200 feet on a flat near Early Winters Creek. 16 miles west of Winthrop near the Early Winters Information Center. Toilets. Water. Fee.

Ballard. 6 units near the Methow River. 7 miles from Mazama. Pit toilets. Water. Fee.

River Bend. 5 units. Turn east on Forest Road 060 about 7 miles from Mazama; campground in 1 mile. Pit toilets. Water. Fee.

Harts Pass. 5 primitive sites in the original camp. 18.5 miles from Mazama. Pit toilets.

Meadows. 14 units in a pleasant loop around an open meadow at 6,300 feet. Turn south at Harts Pass 18.5 miles from Mazama onto Forest Road 500; campground in 0.5 mile. Pit toilets.

HIKES 94–98

Pearrygin Lake State Park. 83 units on open loops near Pearrygin Lake. 5 miles northeast of Winthrop. Restrooms. Water. Electricity. Fee. Reservations.

Falls Creek. 7 units on a forested loop near the Chewuch River. On Forest Road 51 north of Winthrop. Waterfalls nearby. Pit toilets. Water. Fee.

Flat. 7 units on Eightmile Creek. On Forest Road 5130 off Forest Road 51 north of Winthrop. Pit toilets. Water. Fee.

Tiffany Spring. 6 sites at the trailhead to Tiffany Lake. On Forest Road 39 off Forest Road 37 about 25 miles northeast of Winthrop. Pit toilets. Spring water.

Black Pine Lake. 21 units on a pretty, forested mountain lake below Buttermilk Butte. Best route is to drive 11 miles east of Twisp on Black Pine–Twisp River Road to Forest Road 43, across the river to the left. Lake in nearly 8 more miles. Pit toilets. Water. Fee.

MOUNT BAKER HIGHWAY 542: GLACIER TO ARTIST POINT

HIKES 99–105

Douglas Fir. 30 sites, some near the river in shady forest. 2 miles east of Glacier on Highway 542. May be closed during the week. Community kitchen. Restrooms. Water. Fee. Reservations.

Silver Fir. 21 sites mostly along the river. All in a forest setting. 13 miles from Glacier. Sandbars some years provide wading for children. Restrooms. Water. Fee. Reservations.

Hannegan. 6 sites in a trailhead camp for packers. 5 miles from Highway 542, at the end of Hannegan Forest Road 32.

A fawn hidden from predators by camouflage color

APPENDIX 2
INFORMATION SOURCES

Mount Baker–Snoqualmie National Forest
21905 64th Avenue West
Mountlake Terrace, WA 98043
(425) 775-9702

North Bend Ranger Station
42404 SE North Bend Way
North Bend, WA 98045
(425) 888-1421

Darrington Ranger Station
1405 Emmens Street
Darrington, WA 98241
(360) 435-1155

Mount Baker Ranger Station
2105 State Route 20
Sedro-Woolley, WA 98284
(360) 856-5700

SEASONAL CENTERS
Glacier Public Service Center
Glacier, WA 98244
(360) 599-2714

Verlot Public Service Center
33515 Mountain Loop Highway
Granite Falls, WA 98241
(360) 691-7791

Snoqualmie Pass
P.O. Box 17
Snoqualmie Pass, WA 98068
(425) 434-6111

Okanogan–Wenatchee National Forest
215 Melody Lane
Wenatchee, WA 98801
(509) 662-4335

Cle Elum Ranger Station
803 West 2nd Street
Cle Elum, WA 98922
(509) 674-4411

Leavenworth–Lake Wenatchee Ranger Station
600 Sherbourne
Levenworth, WA 98826
(509) 548-6977

Entiat Ranger Station
2108 Entiat Way
P.O. Box 476
Entiat, WA 98822
(509) 784-1511

Chelan Ranger Station
428 West Woodin Avenue
P.O. Box 680
Chelan, WA 98816
(509) 682-2576

Methow Valley Ranger Station
502 Glover
P.O. Box 188
Twisp, WA 98856
(509) 997-2131

SEASONAL CENTERS
Methow Valley Visitor Center
24 West Chewuch Road
Winthrop, WA 98862
(509) 996-4000

NATIONAL PARKS

North Cascades National Park, Ross Lake, and Lake Chelan
  National Recreation Areas
2105 State Route 20
Sedro-Woolley, WA 98284
(360) 856-5700

SEASONAL CENTERS

North Cascades Visitor Center
Newhalem, WA 98283
(206) 386-4495

Wilderness Information Center
Marblemount, WA 98267
(360) 873-4500 (ext. 39)

NATIONAL PARK/FOREST SERVICE CAMPGROUND RESERVATIONS

(877) 444-6777

WASHINGTON STATE PARKS

For current information on campground conditions,
  call (360) 902-8844
For reservations, call (880) CAMPOUT (226-7688)

WEBSITES

Mount Baker–Snoqualmie National Forest
www.fs.fed.us/r6/mbs

Okanogan–Wenatchee National Forest
www.fs.fed.us/r6/Wenatchee

North Cascades National Park
www.nps.gov/noca

FOREST SERVICE INFORMATION CENTER

REI Information Center
222 Yale Avenue North
Seattle, WA 98109
(206) 470-4060

Clark's nutcracker

APPENDIX 3
READING SUGGESTIONS

WILDERNESS TRAVEL

Douglas, William O. *My Wilderness, The Pacific West.* Doubleday & Company, Garden City, NY.

Douglas, William O. *Of Men and Mountains.* Doubleday & Company, Garden City, NY.

Graydon, Don, ed. *Mountaineering, The Freedom of the Hills* (6th ed.). The Mountaineers Books, Seattle, WA.

Manning, Harvey. *Backpacking: One Step at a Time.* Vintage Books, New York, NY.

TREES AND FLOWERS

Arno, Stephen F., and Ramona P. Hammerly. *Northwest Trees.* The Mountaineers Books, Seattle, WA.

Lyons, C. P. *Trees, Shrubs and Flowers to Know in Washington.* J. M. Dent & Sons, Ltd., Vancouver, B.C., Canada.

Manning, Harvey. *Mountain Flowers of the Cascades and Olympics.* The Mountaineers Books, Seattle, WA.

NATURE GUIDES

Kozloff, Eugene N. *Plants and Animals of the Pacific Northwest.* University of Washington Press, Seattle, WA.

Peterson, Roger Tory. *A Field Guide to Western Birds.* Houghton Mifflin Company, Boston, MA.

Whitney, Stephen R. *A Field Guide to the Cascades and Olympics.* The Mountaineers Books, Seattle, WA.

INDEX

ABOUT THE AUTHOR

E. M. Sterling (1920–2001) was born and reared in the Midwest and has lived and hiked in the Pacific Northwest since the 1940s. A veteran outdoorsman and writer, Sterling also wrote *Best Short Hikes in Washington's South Cascades and Olympics*, the companion to this book.

ABOUT THE PHOTOGRAPHER

Photographer and writer Ira Spring's crisp, breathtaking images of the Northwest wilderness have been inspiring outdoor enthusiasts for several decades. His creative stamp can be found on more than forty books on the outdoors, including many in The Mountaineers Books' 100 Hikes in™ series. One of the Northwest's most active trail lobbyists, Spring was given the 1992 Theodore Roosevelt Conservation Award for his volunteer efforts toward trail preservation and funding.

Other titles you might enjoy from The Mountaineers Books

Available at fine bookstores and outdoor stores, by phone at 800-553-4453, or at *www.mountaineersbooks.org*

Best Short Hikes in™ Washington's South Cascades & Olympics by E. M. Sterling. $12.95, paperback. 0-89886-417-8.

Best Hikes with Children in® Western Washington & the Cascades, Volume 1, 2nd Edition, by Joan Burton. $14.95, paperback. 0-89886-564-6.

Best Hikes with Children in® Western Washington & the Cascades, Volume 2, 2nd Edition, by Joan Burton. $14.95, paperback. 0-89886-626-X.

Washington State Parks: A Complete Recreation Guide, 2nd Edition, by Marge and Ted Mueller. $16.95, paperback. 0-89886-642-1

Exploring Washington's Wild Areas: A Guide for Hikers, Backpackers, Climbers, Cross-Country Skiers, and Paddlers, 2nd Edition, by Marge and Ted Mueller. $18.95, paperback. 0-89886-807-6.

100 Classic Hikes in™ Washington by Ira Spring and Harvey Manning. $19.95, paperback. 0-89886-586-7.

Hiking Washington's Geology by Scott Babcock, and Robert J. Carson. $16.95 paperback. 0-89886-548-4.

A Field Guide to the Cascades & Olympics by Stephen Whitney. $18.95, paperback. 0-89886-077-6.

Animal Tracks of the Pacific Northwest by Karen Pandell and Chris Stall. $6.95, paperback. 0-89886-012-1.

Staying Found: The Complete Map & Compass Handbook, 3rd Edition, by June Fleming. $12.95, paperback. 0-89886-785-1.

GPS Made Easy: Using Global Positioning Systems in the Outdoors, 3rd Edition, by Lawrence Letham. $14.95, paperback. 0-89886-802-5.

First Aid: A Pocket Guide, 4th Edition, by Christopher Van Tilburg, M.D. $3.50, paperback. 0-89886-719-3.

Emergency Survival: A Pocket Guide by Christopher Van Tilburg, M.D. $3.50, paperback. 0-89886-768-1.

Everyday Wisdom: 1001 Expert Tips for Hikers by Karen Berger. $16.95, paperback. 0-89886-523-9.

THE MOUNTAINEERS, founded in 1906, is a nonprofit outdoor activity and conservation club, whose mission is "to explore, study, preserve, and enjoy the natural beauty of the outdoors. . . ." Based in Seattle, Washington, the club is now the third-largest such organization in the United States, with 15,000 members and five branches throughout Washington State.

The Mountaineers sponsors both classes and year-round outdoor activities in the Pacific Northwest, which include hiking, mountain climbing, ski-touring, snowshoeing, bicycling, camping, kayaking and canoeing, nature study, sailing, and adventure travel. The club's conservation division supports environmental causes through educational activities, sponsoring legislation, and presenting informational programs. All club activities are led by skilled, experienced volunteers, who are dedicated to promoting safe and responsible enjoyment and preservation of the outdoors.

If you would like to participate in these organized outdoor activities or the club's programs, consider a membership in The Mountaineers. For information and an application, write or call The Mountaineers, Club Headquarters, 300 Third Avenue West, Seattle, WA 98119; 206-284-6310.

The Mountaineers Books, an active, nonprofit publishing program of the club, produces guidebooks, instructional texts, historical works, natural history guides, and works on environmental conservation. All books produced by The Mountaineers Books fulfill the club's mission.

Send or call for our catalog of more than 500 outdoor titles:

The Mountaineers Books
1001 SW Klickitat Way, Suite 201
Seattle, WA 98134
800-553-4453
mbooks@mountaineersbooks.org
www.mountaineersbooks.org

The Mountaineers Books is proud to be a corporate sponsor of Leave No Trace, whose mission is to promote and inspire responsible outdoor recreation through education, research, and partnerships. The Leave No Trace program is focused specifically on human-powered (nonmotorized) recreation.

Leave No Trace strives to educate visitors about the nature of their recreational impacts, as well as offer techniques to prevent and minimize such impacts. Leave No Trace is best understood as an educational and ethical program, not as a set of rules and regulations.

For more information, visit *www.LNT.org*, or call 800-332-4100.